County Maps and Histories Series

Hertfordshire

Valerie G. Scott

and

Tony Rook

Quiller Press

A view of St Albans Abbey by J. Cartwright engraved after G.R. Arnold, 1798. (By courtesy of the British Library)

Quiller Press Ltd., 46 Lillie Road,
London SW6 1TN.

First Published 1989

Copyright © 1989 caption text: Valerie G. Scott
history text: Tony Rook

ISBN 1 870948 20 3

County Maps & Histories

Hertfordshire

Valerie G. Scott and Tony Rook.

A ntique maps are an ideal medium through which to view history. They show the changing landscape, the different social patterns of the period in which they were made, the coming of the canals and railways which had such a significant effect on people's lives, and the country homes of the rich and famous. The continuing fascination of an old map is that the more you study it, the more information it reveals. In other words, to love old maps is to love history and vice-versa.

Robert Louis Stevenson summed this up in *Treasure Island* when he said, 'I am told that there are people who do not care for maps, and find it hard to believe. The names, the shapes . . . the courses of the roads and rivers . . . are an inexhaustible fund of interest for any man with eyes to see or two-penceworth of imagination to understand with.'

It is surprising that in the past old maps have not been used more by historians. In this book on Hertfordshire, the fourth in a comprehensive series on the counties of Great Britain, we hope to right this by combining history and maps. By doing this we follow in the footsteps of the very early mapmakers many of whom systematically surveyed – often under appallingly difficult circumstances – and drew up maps of every county and then collated them into atlases. The antique maps, which we illustrate, are taken from some of the most beautiful originals in existence. They come from collections in map libraries, in private hands, and in antique map galleries, and gratitude must go to those who have allowed us to handle and photograph them.

The first county ever called 'The Garden of England' was Hertfordshire. Thomas Fuller coined the phrase in *Worthies of England* in 1622. He called it the garden of England *for delight*. It is particularly the garden of London, for it provides the countryside that Londoners have sought out through the centuries. As Kipling said "such gardens are not made by singing: 'Oh! How beautiful!' and sitting in the shade". Here men have toiled, armies have marched and battles have been fought; Caesar accepted the surrender of the Britons and William I of the English.

On a journey through Hertfordshire in the 'fair and warm' summer of 1822, William Cobbett wrote, 'What that man ever invented under the name of pleasure grounds can equal these fields in Hertfordshire!' In these fields were sown seeds which have yielded harvests throughout the world. No other county has given both a Cardinal and a Pope to the Church of Rome. The first British martyr, Saint Alban, was a Hertfordshire man and on the site of his mar-tyrdom was created the earliest monastic establishment in western Europe, St Albans abbey. It housed one of the most important libraries in medieval times.

At St Albans, Parliament was conceived in the Council which drafted the greatest document of liberty, Magna Carta, in 1213, and born with the Model Parliament in 1295. In Hertfordshire Thomas Clarkson, who was responsible for the foundation of the Anti-Slavery Society, resolved to devote his life to the abolition of the slave trade and it was Hertfordshire protest which led to witchcraft being banished from the statute book. From the county the seeds of freedom and democracy have been carried all over the world. A vicar of Ware became the first President of Harvard College; William Gordon, said to have been Private Secretary to George Washington, was the first historian of the United States, and Samuel Stone, from Hertford, founded Connecticut. Cecil Rhodes, son of a vicar of Bishop's Stortford, became one of the most important statesmen in South Africa and created Rhodesia, now Zim-babwe.

This quiet, rural county has a place in the history of technology. Here the first canal lock was built, and the idea of a national canal system conceived. The first turnpike road was in Hertfordshire; also through it passes the first main-line railway from London and the first motorway. Scientific agriculture and chemical fertilisers originated here and Henry Bessemer, who invented a steel-making process, was born near Hitchin.

The county has sheltered and inspired literary figures too numerous to list, including George Chapman, who translated Homer (and inspired Keats), Thomas More, Francis Bacon, Izaac Walton, the gentle and compleat ang-ler, who fished in the River Lea, Charles Lamb *alias* Elia, William Cowper, the well-known English poet, Lord Lyt-ton, the novelist who often entertained contemporary writ-ers including Charles Dickens at his home at Knebworth House; E.M. Forster, George Orwell and George Bernard Shaw.

Kings, queens, princes and princesses have enjoyed the Hertfordshire air. At King's Langley the royal palace was the residence of Edwards I, II and III and the scene of part of the action in Shakespeare's *Richard II*. Henry VIII spent much of his time in the county and his children Edward, Mary and Elizabeth rode south from it to London to their coronations. James I had a palace at Theobalds and a hunt-ing lodge at Royston. Richard III and Charles I rode from

Hertfordshire, the former to die at Bosworth and the latter to raise his standard at Nottingham. Queen Elizabeth, the Queen Mother, was born at St Paul's Walden, and Princess Margaret and the future Queen Elizabeth II often stayed there.

It comes as no surprise that Hertfordshire is the birthplace of the quiet green revolution that changed our concept of town planning – the Garden City movement – and the first New Towns created after the war.

Hertfordshire's face is one of rural plenty and natural peace, but a large part of its charm lies in its ever-present sense of the past. 'You can scarcely walk a mile anywhere,' said Sir William Beach Thomas "without acquiring some sense of the rich continuity of its history and its wholly English character."

County Origins

The origins of the county of Hertford are obscure. Its name is first recorded in the eleventh century, but it is likely that it started as an administrative district of the fortress town of Hertford created by Edward the Elder in 912. Even after the changes that took place in 1965 its boundaries seem pretty arbitrary. For example, the border almost runs along the bottom of the scarp slope of the Chilterns, the range of hills which form the northern edge of the London basin – but in some places it bends further north, while in others it yields territory to Bedfordshire or Buckinghamshire. In 1824 a letter in the county archive records:

> 'The Justices request me to make a return of the property in the Hamlet of St Thomas' Chapel (Meppershall) which is out of my power to do, as the counties of Hertford and Bedford are so intermixed with one another that no one knows how to divide them . . .'

The county boundary went right through the rectory! Inscribed on a beam in the parlour was: 'If you would sit in Hertfordshire then draw your chair near the fire.'

Royston, a market town created by a priory at a crossroads in 1189 without consideration of invisible boundaries, was in five parishes until given single parish status in 1540, and remained in both Hertfordshire and Cambridgeshire until 1897. It is easily recognised as an odd bump in the county boundary at the north-eastern corner of the modern map.

Part of the division between the county and Essex more or less follows the river Lea, which was once the frontier between the English and the Danes, but it forsakes this historic line at Hoddesdon to follow the river Stort as far as

---

'Hartfordiae Comitatus', 1577 by Christopher Saxton

This map of Hertfordshire is extremely important as it was made from an original survey by cartographer Christopher Saxton, the first man to survey and map the counties of England and Wales. It appeared in an atlas published in 1579 containing all the counties of England and Wales with a frontispiece showing a regal portrait of Elizabeth I. Saxton, who has been called the 'father of English cartography' is said to have 'travelled the whole of England through towns and villages for nine continuous years with the utmost labour and industry and not only drew the counties separately and most carefully, but took the pains to have them engraved in bronze tablets . . . .' Although his maps do not show roads (they were not important in those days as few people travelled far afield) his maps are surprisingly accurate in their detail of towns, rivers and geographical features. Saxton's maps were copied again and again by later mapmakers. (By courtesy of the British Library, London)

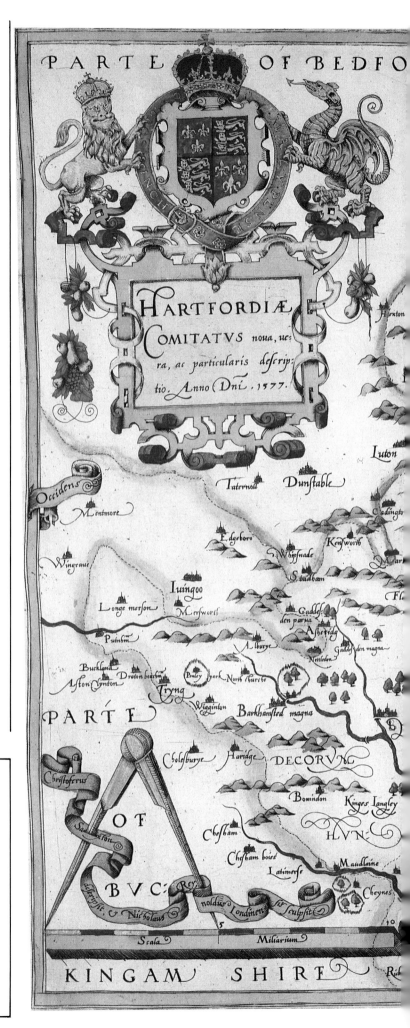

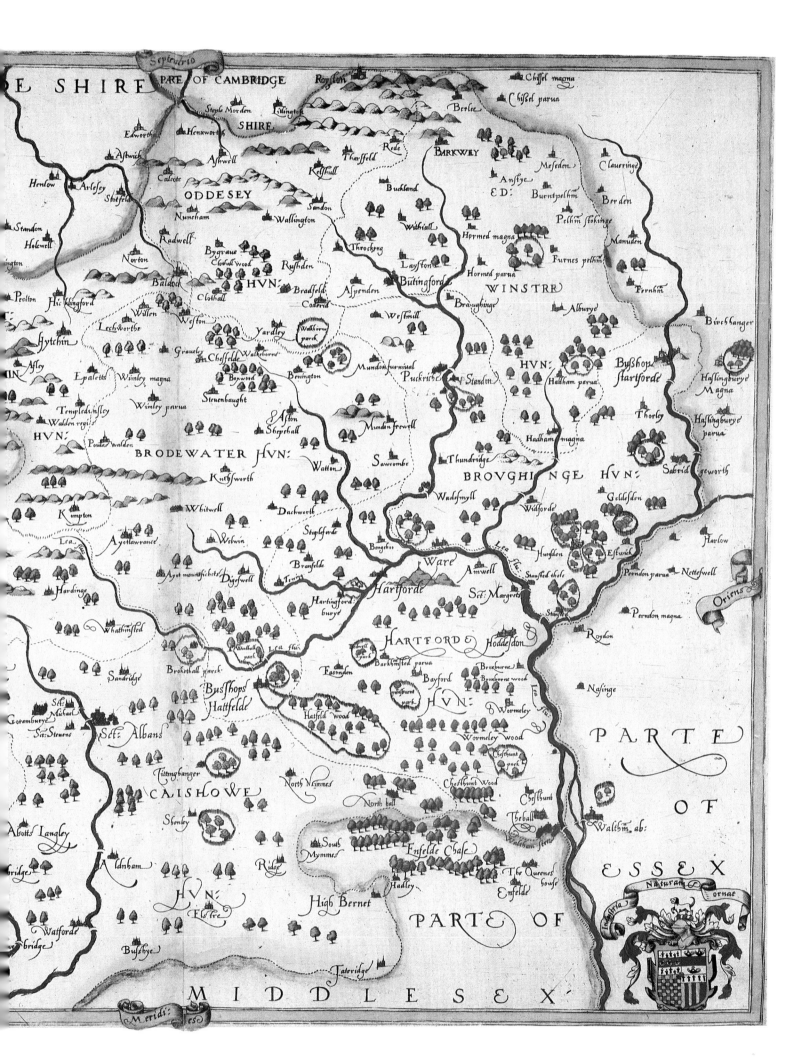

E SHIRE PARE OF CAMBRIDGE   Royston   Chissel magna

Chissel parua

Steple Morden   Lillington   Berlee

Edworth   Henxworth   SHIRE

Astwick   Ashwell   Rede   BARKWEY   Meseden   Claueringe

Henlow   Arlesey   Calcote   Tharffeld   Anstye   Burntpelhm   Berden

Stotfeld   ODDESEY   Kelfhull   Buckland   ED: Pelhm stokinge

Standon   Nuneham   Wallington   Sandon   Withiall   Hormed magna   Manuden

Holewell   Radwell   Throckng   Hormed parua   Furnes pelhm

ington   Norton   Bygraue   Rushden   Layston   Fernhm

Pecston   Clothall wood   Butingford   WINSTRR

Hicklingford   Baldock   HVN: Bradfeld   Aspenden   Braughinge   Alburye   Birchhanger

Willen   Clothall   Coderid   Westmill

hytchin   Weston   Yardley   Walkhorne parck

Lechworthe   Graueley   Chessfelde   Walkhorne   Mundon furniuall   Puckrich   Standon   HVN: Bysshop startforde

Asley   Brunington   Haslingburye Magna

IN   Epaletts   Wimley magna   Benwood   Hadham parua

Templedinsley   Wimley parua   Steuenhaught   Mundon frewell   Thorley   Haslingburye parua

Walden regis   Aston   Shephall   Hadham magna

HVN: Poules walden   Sawcombe   Thundridge   Sabridgeworth

BRODEWATER HVN: Watton   BROVGHINGE HVN:

Kempton   Knthsworth   Wadesmyll   Widsforde   Geddesden

Whitwell   Dachworth   Harlow

Lea flu: Ayotlawrance   Welwin   Stapleforde   Hunsden   Estwick

Hardinge   Bengehoo   Lea flu: Perndon parua   Netteswell

Ayot mounsichets   Digeswell   Branfelde   Stansted thele   Oriens

Tewing   Ware   Amwell   Stansted

Whathmsted   Hartforde   Sct: Margrets   Perndon magna

Hartingford burye   HARTFORDE   Hoddesdon   Roydon

Sct: Gorambury   Welhall parck   HARTFORDE   Bayford   Broxburne   Nasinge

Sct: Steuens   Brokethall parck   Essenden   Barhmsted parua   Broxburne wood

Sandridge   Bysshops Hattfelde   gronsburnt park   HVN: Wormeley

Sct: Albans   Hatsfeld wood   Wormeley wood   Chesthunt park

Tittnghanger   North Nymmes   Chesthunt Wood   PARTE

Abotts Langley   CAISHOWE   North hall   Chesthunt   OF

Shenley   South Mymmes   Theball   Waltham ab:

ridge   Aldnham   Ridge   Enfelde Chase   Waltham streete   ESSEX

HVN: Hadley   The Queenes howse

Elstre   High Bernet   Enfelde

Watforde   PARTE OF

rbridge   Busshye   Tateridge

MIDDLESEX

Industria Naturam Ornat

V

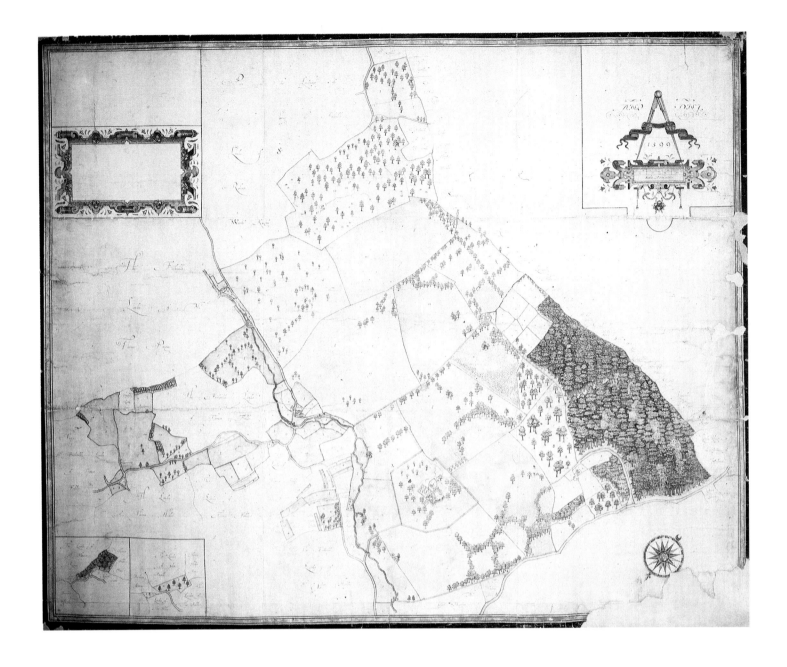

Bishop's Stortford. Prior to 1576 one High Sheriff served for both Essex and Hertfordshire. 'The said several counties were not then well inhabited with gentlemen of good ability to serve the said office as, thanks to God, they be at present,' ran the preamble to the Act of Queen Elizabeth I which created the new post. 'Keepers of the Peace' had been appointed by Edward III in 1327. The authority of these 'Justices', or Magistrates as they came to be known, grew, as did their number, until, landowners and wealthy gentlemen to a man, they virtually ruled the county by the eighteenth century. Exactly a hundred years ago the County Council, an elected body, took over their administrative functions.

The character of Hertfordshire has always been deter-

mined by the fact that it is the rural area north of London. Until recent times people earned their living either by growing produce, mostly for the London market, or by providing services for travellers passing through on their way to and from the capital. For much of its history the owners of most of the country houses have been professional men with businesses in the City, rather than hereditary nobility. The modern commuter continues a long tradition.

The landscape is always domestic, never dramatic, yet it varies greatly from place to place; there is no one spot that is typically Hertfordshire. Arthur Young, first Secretary of the Board of Agriculture, wrote, in 1805:

'The truth is that the soils of this county mix and run into each other in a remarkable manner.'

This is mainly the effect of glaciation. The underlying geology is simple. The county is spread on a great slab of chalk which slopes upwards to the north-west, culminating in the ridge of the Chilterns, some 600 feet high. Covering the chalk, in the south-east, lies a layer of 'tertiary deposits', mostly London clay, which has little value for agriculture.

The river Thames once flowed just north of the London clay, on a line joining Watford and Ware. During the second (Anglian) Ice Age, the ice front pushed over the north-east end of the Chilterns, reducing their height, and flowing behind them into the proto-Thames valley. Polar bears

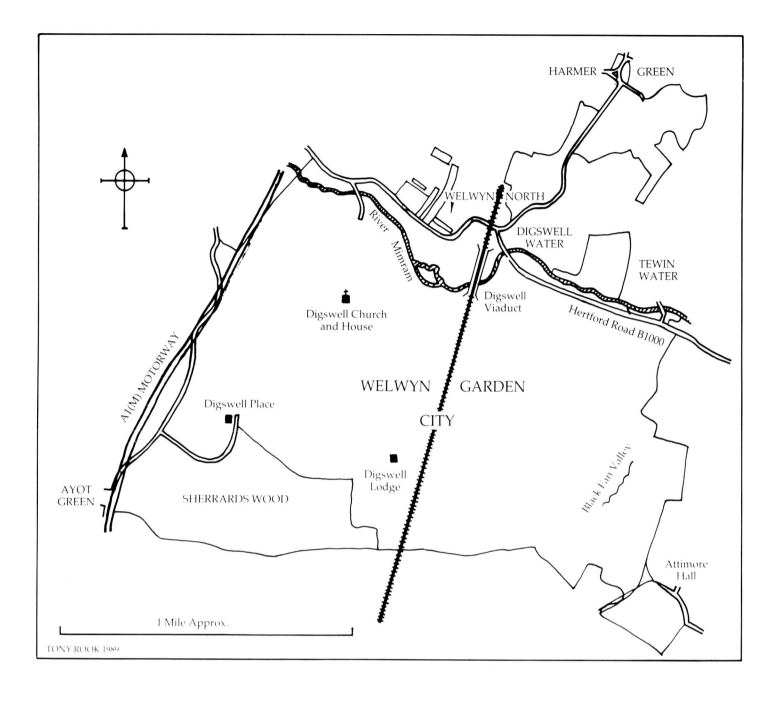

Welwyn Garden City map. Places shown: HARMER GREEN, WELWYN NORTH, DIGSWELL WATER, TEWIN WATER, River Mimram, Digswell Viaduct, Hertford Road B1000, Digswell Church and House, A1(M) MOTORWAY, WELWYN GARDEN CITY, Digswell Place, Black Fan Valley, AYOT GREEN, SHERRARDS WOOD, Digswell Lodge, Attimore Hall, 1 Mile Approx.

TONY ROOK 1989

paraded and penguins paddled at Park Street, while Ware and Hertford were deep frozen under a great grey glacier. The proto-Thames formed a lake, and finally cut the valley through which it now flows. When the ice retreated the old Thames valley was marked by a broad band of gravel across the county and the area formerly under the glacier was covered by a spread of 'chalky boulder clay' which the ice had contained.

Apart from small but important areas of gault clay in the north, where the county boundary runs north of the Chilterns, the surface geology of Hertfordshire can be divided into four main areas. In the north and west is chalk with thin, well-drained soils covered by patches of well-wooded 'clay with flints' left behind as the chalk was dissolved over the ages by rain. In the north-east are the heavy but very fertile soils based on boulder clay – the 'champion country' famous for its barley. A band across the map from Watford to Ware contains large towns and, significantly, modern gravel pits. South of the gravel the soils are acid and the ground heavy. This area, once used by woodland industries and for pasture and meadow, is today marked by the golf courses and semi-detached houses of surburbia.

The effects of the diversion of the Thames can clearly be seen in the behaviour of the river Lea, which flows south-east down the dip slope of the chalk as far as Hatfield. Here it is caught by the old river valley, and flows north-east as far as Ware before finding its way, down the track of another lobe of the glacier, to the modern Thames. This has an important effect on the development of the county because Hertford, the county town, although strategically sited on the river, was actually further from London than Ware, which has as a result always been more important commercially.

Early Settlers

Finds among the gravels and along the river valleys tell us that hunter-gatherers were active in the Old and Middle Stone Ages over most of the county. The farmers of the New Stone, Bronze and Early Iron Ages preferred the easily-cultivated chalk. The 'Icknield Way belt' is thickly covered by prehistoric sites and monuments.

The first settlers on the gravel belt belonged to the pre-Roman Belgic tribe, the Catuvellauni. Between the Ver and the Lea they dug a massive frontier ditch, part of which can still be seen as the impressive Beech Bottom Dyke, St Albans. They also built a 100-acre fortified enclosure at Wheathampstead. Caesar describes the *oppidum* (fortified place) of his enemy Cassivellaunus as 'protected by forests and marshes . . . of great natural strength and excellently fortified'. Devil's Dyke, Wheathampstead, fits this description.

A century after Caesar, the Romans returned to rule the Britons, who had been trading with the Empire for generations, and, locally at least, were mainly welcomed. Roman roads radiated from the bridgehead on the Thames, and London grew there almost by accident, establishing a pattern which was permanently to affect the county. The main road to the north, Ermine Street, went up the Lea valley; Akeman Street went north-west through the Tring gap in the Chilterns. Between the two went Watling Street, and on it the Romans created the town Verulamium, with its special status of *municipium* – probably as a capital for Adminius, the British prince of the blood who had been expelled by his father Cunobelinus for pro-Roman sympathies in 40 AD.

It is not surprising that Verulamium was destroyed in the rebellion led by Boadicea in 61 AD, along with London and Colchester. A new town grew from the ashes, however, with a forum, dedicated in 79 AD, which had a *basilica* (town hall) comparable in size with the present Abbey. How this must have impressed the hut-dwelling natives!

The only main Roman roads 'across' the county were that from Verulamium to Colchester via Puckeridge, and the prehistoric track of the Icknield Way running along the line of the Chilterns. Small towns grew or were created, at (or near) Cow Roast, Brockley Hill, Welwyn, Puckeridge, Royston, Ware and Baldock. Most of them were to disappear in the Dark Ages. Villas were built, often on or close to the sites of native farms, mostly combining the functions of country house and farm. They were inhabited by generations of native Britons who had become Romans, but few Hertfordshire villas reached any great heights of luxury.

What happened after the collapse of Roman administration in the fifth century is a puzzle. We do know that Verulamium public works went on – a water main was laid in the latter part of the century. There was a strong Christian tradition too – St Germanus came to the city in 429 AD and visited the tomb of St Alban.

There were also Saxon settlers along the Icknield Way at this time and they reached Verulamium by the end of the sixth century.

When the first Danish pirates arrived at the end of the eighth century, England consisted of a number of warring Saxon kingdoms. The invaders began to overwinter in England, and in 865 AD a great army landed in East Anglia with the aim of conquest and settlement. Northumbria, Mercia

'Hertfordia Comitatus' by Joan Blaeu, 1645

At the beginning of the seventeenth century Amsterdam was one of the most important centres for trade in Europe, partly because it was the hub of the banking and diamond industry and partly because it was the base for the powerful Dutch East India Company. Publishing, therefore, also flourished and the Blaeu family firm was founded by Willem Janszoon Blaeu who produced a wealth of maps, globes, sea charts and other works. The cartographer of this map was Joan Blaeu, son of Willem, who carried on the business after the death of his father. It appeared in a six-volume work, Theatrum Orbis Terrarum. *A disastrous fire destroyed the Blaeu premises in 1672 and Joan died the following year. All the Blaeu maps are highly decorative and beautifully engraved and Hertfordshire is no exception. (By courtesy of the British Library)*

ORIENSIS
TVS

Part Septentrio of Cambridge Shire

ODSEY HVND.

HITCHING HVNDRED

BROADWATER HVND.

EDWINSTRE HVND.

BRAGHING HVND.

ESSEX

HARTFORD HVND.

ESSEXIÆ

PARS.

CAISHO HVND.

HONI SOIT QVI MAL Y PENSE

MIDDLESEX.

Milliaria Anglica quorum quatuor unum Germanicum.

Meridies.

ix

and East Anglia fell to them. Only Wessex resisted but, under Alfred, the English defeated them. The Danish king, along with twenty-nine of his chiefs, was baptised and became Christian.

A frontier was established between the English and the Danes. It ran along the river Lea, dividing the present county in two. It did not separate different peoples so much as different customs and laws. Strangely enough, this line also divides the area in the west, which had contained most of the Roman villas, from the rest of the county, and many scholars in different disciplines note that there has always been some sort of division here.

In 895 AD the *Anglo-Saxon Chronicle* records that the Danes brought their ships up the Lea and built a fort twenty miles above London. Alfred 'rode along the river and looked to see where the river could be blocked so that they would not be able to bring their ships out: this they proceeded to do: they made two forts on either side of the river, but when they had just begun the host saw that they could not bring out their ships. Thereupon they abandoned them and escaped across country.'

It is said that Alfred also blocked the river with an obstruction from which Ware derives its name. Until recently local people pronounced the name as 'Weir'. In 912 AD the *Anglo-Saxon Chronicle* tells us his son Edward the Elder established a fortress at Hertford. This is the first time the county town is mentioned by name.

Feudal Herts

Instead of laying siege to London after he had defeated Harold at Hastings in 1066, William the Conqueror advanced right round the city, burning towns and laying to waste the countryside. The English surrendered at Little Berkhampstead.

To subdue the Saxons, William I built strong castles at strategic places. There were three in Hertfordshire, at Berkhamsted on Akeman Street to guard the Tring Gap, at Hertford, on the site of Alfred's burgh to dominate the river valleys and Ermine Street, and at Bishop's Stortford on Stane Street.

Under Norman rule, all land belonged to the king and

'Hartford shire Described' by John Speed, 1676
At the top left of this map is a plan of the county town, Hertford, and at the top right a plan of Verulamium, the Roman city extensively excavated by Sir Mortimer Wheeler in the early 1930s. The dedications on the coats-of-arms are to Roger, Earl of Clare and Hertford and Edward Seymour, Earl of Hertford. The engraver of the map was the Dutchman Jodocus Hondius. The map appeared in Speed's work Theatre of the Empire of Great Britaine. *Note that there are still no roads shown and the county is divided into hundreds, the names of which are still reflected in places such as Dacorum and Hitchin today. John Speed is undoubtedly England's best known cartographer but although his maps are very attractive they are based on the work of other mapmakers rather than on an original survey. He admitted this when he said, 'I have put my sickle into other men's corn'. But this is not to detract from the great contribution he made to cartography; his maps were still being issued nearly 200 years after his death. Speed was born at Farndon, Cheshire and was a tailor by trade but his great passion was for history. He was supported in his atlas and history projects (he also produced a history of Great Britain) by Sir Fulke Greville who obtained permission from Queen Elizabeth I for him to work from the Custom House in London. (By courtesy of Valerie Scott)*

HARTFORD SHIRE DESCRIBED

The fituations of Hartford, and the moft an:
cient towne s Albons with fuch memorable actions as have happened

VEROLANIUM

PART OF

Part of Cambridge Shire.   Royfton

Little Chefill   Great Chefill

fteple Mordent   Barley   Newfels   Minffagbery Abbetfbery Cokenhatch   Claueing

Edworth   Henxworth   The Beacon   Reede   Kelfhull   Tharfield   Guggng   Meffden Anfte   Burnt Pelham   Beaches

Afhwell   Calkott   ODSEY   Odfey Grange   HUNDRED   fanden   Buckland   Great Hormed   Pelham furniie   Little Hormed   Stokenpellam   Helffams hall

Radwell   Nennham   Wallington   Bigrave   Hidehall   EDWINSTRE   HUNDR.   Redſwells   what barnes   Mulforde

Norton   Rufhden   Quickfwood   Throcking Beachams   Alſwick   Adbery hall   Graueſend

Baldock   Bradfield   Cotteral   Layſton   Cormgley   Owley   Quenbery   Adbery   Patmerhall

Wilton   Darnells   Clothall   Kingſwoodbery   Pannis   Buntingford   Waymer caſtle   Kickerell

Letchworth   Camberlew Gorne   Yardley   Weſtmill   Braghing   Bifhops Stortford

Greatwimley   Graueley   Weſton   Walkerne   Haultwick   Standon   Hadhamenagh   Spellbrooke

The Beacon   Box   Woode   Benington   Finchcrende   Munden furmmall   Fryers   Upſhall   Little Hadham   Thorely

The Priory   Littlewimley   Halmley   Munden fre well   Dane ende   Satridge   Great Hadham   Tednambu   Sabſworth

Temple Dinſley   BROADWATER   Afhton   HUNDRED.   Sawcomb   Colliers end   Berwick   Bartrams   Caſtullbery   Shingle hall   Hidehall

Langley   Broadwater   Shepehale   Woodhall   High Croſe   Thundridg   BRAGHING HUNDRED   Peſtebery

THE CATEWCHLANS   Brighterende   Tunwell   Burwghs grene   Newhall   Bleakſbeay   Geldeſden   New place

Howeende   Knebworth   Watton   Temple   Rearch   Wadeſmill   Widſford   Mollocks   Hunſfon   Eaſhwike   Harlow

Cudicot   Wulmergrene   Gabbins   Rikneſhe   Waee parks   Wilburs hill

Avet Laurence   Welwyne   Stapleford   Waterford hall   Benge   Wideford   Stanſted   Little Prenden   Briggens

Bibſwell   Digſwell   Branfield   The Scale Pantaunger   Ware   Amwell   Margret   Great Prenden

Kenmere   Little Avor   Tewing   Mereden   The Beacon   Ataly   Iſdley   Southchele

Ware   Hartfingfey   Hart ford   Little Amwell   Stauthcele   Roydon

Ludwik hall   HARTFORD HUNDRED   The Ree

Brokelhall   Helwell   Hodidon   Naſing

Eafenden   Barkhampsted   Reyford   Broxebourne   The Ba   Weed

St. Albans   Sanrtridge   Bedwell park   Pauſbowne   Wormeley

Bythops flatfeld   Popes   Wormeley   ESSEX

Beamonds   Shepeſhide   Marpifſeild hall   Newgateſtret   Cheſton park   Cheſton Nunery

NTVM   Sopwell   Northay   Cheſton   Woole Grene   Cheſton Nunery

Hatfeild woode   North Myms   Gabbins   Numhall   Thyebald

Titten hanger   Colney   Nowbarne   Salsbery   Pourells   Pottrels bare   Northhay   Cuhoflgate

CAISHO HUNDRED   Sheuley   Rydge   Gladmore   South Myms   Waltham Abbey

welde   Aldnam   Bynet feild   Hadley   Enfeilde Chace   Waltham Crofs

Cathebery   Elſtree   Bourmehall   High Bernet   Enfeild houſe   Enfeild

Bufhye   Sulloniaca   Eaſt Bernet   Edmunton

Sinklees   Brokeler Hills   Totteridge   Edmunton

MIDDLESEX

In this Countie at three feverall tymes, three mortall and bloody Battells of Englands ciuill diffenfions haue bene fought: The firſt whereof chanced the 23 of Maye Anno 1455. in the towne of St Albons by Richard Duke of Yorke, with his affociats, the Earls of Warwick, and Saleſbury, and Lords of fam conbridg, and Cobham, againſt King H 6. In whos defence Edmund Duke of Somerſet, Henry Earl of Northumberland, and Iohn Lord Clifford with 5000 more loſt their liues, the king himſelfe was wounded in the neck with an arrowe, the Duke of Buckingham and Lorde Sudley in their faces. Humfrey Earle Stafford in his right hand, and the Earle Dorſet alſo ſlaine. On the Dukes part only 600. were ſlaine. The king by them was brought to London, and a reconciliation made by their aduancements vnto dignities and offices.

The ſecound Battell was likewiſe fought in the towne of S. Albons by Queene Margaret, againſt the Duke of Norfolke, and Suffolke; the Earls of Warwick, and Arundell, that by force kept with them the king her huſband, with whome by conſtraynt he held, and on their ſyde foughte vntill the feild was loſt and the Lords fled, when with great ioye he was receiued by his Queene and younge ſone Prince Edward this Battell fell the 17. of February being Shroueſtueſday Anno 1461.

The thrid and laſt battell was fought nere vnto the towne of high Barnet vpon the 14. of Aprill being Eaſter daye, by the Earles of Warwick, and Oxford, and Marques Montacule againſt King Ed. 4. whoe led with him king H 6. his priſoner vnto that feild, and obtayned that daye the victorye againſt his enemyes. There were ſlaine in this bloody Battel Richard Neuill the Stout Earle of Warwick with his brother the Marques and the Earle of Oxford put to flight, & the Duke of Exceſter ſore wounded, and leeft in the feild for dead. On King Edwards part were ſlaine, the Lords Cromwell, Boucher, and Barnes. And on Both parts the number of tenn thouſand men. Anno 1471.

Old: Verolam, the ancient ſeat of Caffebelane, which th his owne libertie he loſt, vnto Caius Iulius Cæſar: was ſometime a citie of great renowne, and of the Romanes, held in great regard who Tacitus tearmeth a free-towne and one of the richeſt in the land: Wherin hath bene found, both pillers, pauements and Romiſh Coynes, moſt certaine toknes of their abode: The river Lea diminiſhed much from the greatnes, which once it bare) was her ſouth defence, and meetes the ruines of thoſe down-caſt walls, in Eaſt and Weſt: Whoſe tract, and trench, as yet apparantly remanes, and extends by meaſure 1270 paſſes: Heere S. Albane Britaines firſt Steph, under Dioclefian, ſuffred martyrdome. Anno 293. Whoſe memoriall great Offa conrinewed by buildings in the place of his execution, a moſt magnificent Abbey: And there alſo Verolams ruines hath rayſed the beautie of now S Albanes.

1 2 3 4 5 6 7 8 9 10

xi

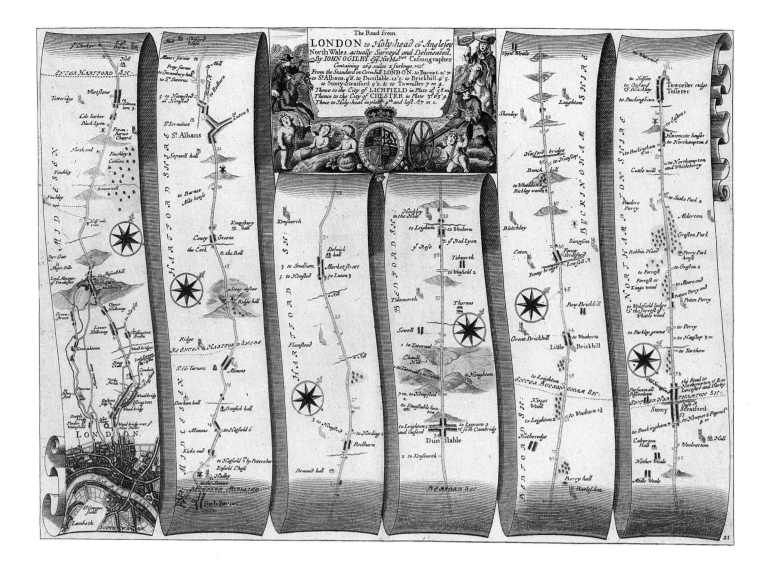

estates were held by strong men, loyal to the king, who paid by homage, taxes and military service. It was inevitable that, under William's successors, some lords built themselves castles, often without royal consent. There are remains of castles at Therfield, Benington, Anstey, Pirton, Wymondley and Walkern, and one is recorded at Wheathampstead, although the site is not known.

In 1086, for the purposes of taxation and administration, William commissioned the first detailed survey of England – the *Domesday Book*. For the first time we are given a picture of the whole county. It is not complete, concerning itself little with towns, counting only men – and even then not all of them. Neither is it exact; areas of land are usually rounded-off to the nearest five 'hides' and even a hide was not an exact area, but the land needed for the upkeep of one household.

The Domesday survey made use of divisions of the county called 'hundreds', which existed before the invasion. One explanation of their origin is that each contained one hundred hides and could contain one hundred households. Under the Saxon system of 'tithing' one man was responsible for the behaviour of ten households, and represented them at a 'hundred moot', a court at which the

King's Reeve (an official of high rank) presided. (We still use the expression 'a moot point' about something open to discussion.) The importance of hundreds slowly declined as manors and parishes took over their roles and Justices replaced Reeves. District councils are the descendents of the hundred system and parishes continued to be listed in their hundreds until recent times and were marked on maps until this century. They were often named from the moot place where the court was held, like Edwin's Tree, the Broad Water. Cashio, a peculiar collection of parishes scattered over the county, consisted of the holdings of the Abbey, and was at first referred to as 'Albanestou Hundret' in 1165, but 'Kaysho', anglicised to 'Kaysford' by 1287. The Hundred known as 'Danais' of the Danes, was latinised to 'Dacorum' by 1196.

Domesday allows us to make a reasonable guess at the size and distribution of the population of the county at the time. Saxon *vills* – it would give the wrong impression to call them villages, since each consisted of a scattered number of hamlets – crowded together on the boulder clay in the north-east where the majority of plough lands are noted. The western chalklands, once rich in villas, were now thinly inhabited and covered in forest, the survey showing large herds of pigs feeding in the woods and few vills with small populations. One hundred and sixty-eight settlements are recorded in Hertfordshire and we can deduce between 20,000 and 30,000 people.

The city of St Albans, the county's most famous historic town, grew up in the late Saxon and Norman periods. St Alban was a citizen of Verulamium who died for the christ-

IOH. OGILVIUS.

Seventeenth century mapmaker, John Ogilby (1600-1675) who claimed to have surveyed and measured all the roads of England and Wales, produced one of the first road books ever to be published entitled Britannia: Volume The First. *His maps were in the form of strips (a format still used by the AA today) like this one showing the route from London to Holyhead (left). The third strip along goes through the Hertfordshire towns of Barnet, St Albans, Redbourn and Dunstable. Ogilby was the first to establish the standard mile of 1,760 yards. He was a colourful character who took up cartography late in life after a variety of careers including dancing master and theatre owner. His first publishing business was destroyed in the Great Fire of London, 1666, but he built it up again and was appointed Royal Cosmographer to Charles II. The portrait is reproduced by kind permission of Map Collector Publications Ltd.*

widened here to form a small lake, were the remains of the walled Roman town of Verulamium. Above the lake on the east side was a fortified town created by the Saxons, a burgh belonging to the king, on the site now known as Kingsbury and the Abbey, with a small group of houses around it, stood south-east of Kingsbury, about a quarter of a mile outside its defences.

Successive abbots developed the settlement by the Abbey into a town and destroyed its competitors. In 948 Abbot Ulsinus built three churches around the Abbey church. At two of them, St Michael's and St Stephen's, travellers on the Roman road, Watling Street, were diverted to miss the Roman town and to pass the Abbey, where a new market was built with the third Church, St Peter's, at its north end. Over the years the Roman city was systematically demolished for building materials. Ulsinus' successors set about the destruction of Kingsbury. They drained its fishpool, which was a main source of its income, bought the burgh from King Aethelraed and demolished all but a token earthwork, which was finally removed in 1152, in the reign of Stephen.

The first Norman Abbot, Paul de Caen, dismissing the Saxon church as *'rudes et idiotas'* began building the great Abbey in its place in about 1077. It was consecrated thirty-nine years later, under Abbot Albini. It was a place of pilgrimage, became one of the most important religious houses in the country, and took precedence over Westminster, thanks to a decision made by the only English Pope, Adrian IV, who was born at Abbots Langley, nearby.

There were forty-six burgesses of St Albans by 1086. Since the new town was created by the Abbey, they were tenants of the Abbot, not the King. This fact was to affect the area in future centuries when the inhabitants sought rights, privileges and representation which were denied. During the fourteenth century they were often in dispute with the Abbey, which maintained that they came under its jurisdiction. In 1327 the townsmen laid seige to the Abbey and were granted a Charter. There was open conflict and legal confusion, and five years later the town paid 'due suit' and a substantial fine to the Abbot.

Hertford was to some extent protected by having a castle which was a royal residence, and by its strategic position, or it too might have suffered the fate of Kingsbury. As it was, the inhabitants of Ware, by their location, were always able to intercept the main goods route to London from Hertford, the river Lea, and, quite literally, to forestall the county town with their own market, officially opened in 1199. During the Middle Ages, referred to as 'Hertford by Ware', the royal borough was 'rather a village'.

Successive cartographers and geographers have remarked on the contrast between Ware and Hertford. The cartographer, John Speed, wrote in 1611: 'Hertford, though the Shire Town is not the richest; the passage through Ware hath left her ways untrodden,' and George Bickham, a cartographer in the mid-eighteenth century: 'The Shire Town, formerly famous, has lost much of its ancient grandeur to Ware through which now runs the great North Road and from whence there is good navigation to London.'

In 1213 a Council was called at St Albans which included, as well as lords temporal and spiritual, the Reeve and four men from each township on the royal estates. This extension of the principle of the ancient moot, or representative court, to a national body was an important step in the development of a democratic parliament. The result of the council's deliberations was one of the most important documents in the establishment of the rule of law: the draft of *Magna Carta*.

The period which followed the signing of *Magna Carta* was a hard one for the people of the county. The King's

ian faith. Modern scholarship dismisses much of the legend that surrounds his death but cannot deny that the first British martyr was executed on a hill across the river Ver from the Roman city. The event probably occurred in 209 AD under the Emperor Geta. In Bede's day, at the beginning of the eighth century, a church 'of wonderful workmanship' marked the site of the martyrdom, the focus of the oldest monastic foundation in western Europe.

At the beginning of the tenth century there were three settlements nearby. On the west of the river Ver, which mercenary army and the Dauphin's army, that had come to the aid of the barons, both ravaged the countryside indiscriminately making the thirteenth century a lawless period.

Despite the troubled times, market towns were created in addition to the Domesday boroughs at Hertford, Berkhamsted, Ashwell, St Albans and Stansted. Baldock was established by the Knights Templars in 1140, Royston in 1189 by the Priors, Chipping Barnet by the Abbey of St Alban, and Ware by the Earl of Leicester, both in 1199. There were about thirty markets by the end of the thirteenth century.

In 1295 St Albans was the venue of the Model Parliament to which every city, borough and main town sent two representatives. 'What touches all must be approved by all' ran the summons.

Edward II frequently kept court at the Royal Estate at King's Langley, and gave his favourite, Gaveston, Berkhamsted in 1308. When the Barons met at Dunstable to enforce the Ordainers' demands, which included the banishment of Gaveston, a papal envoy, sent to mediate, was lodged at St Albans, and met the Barons at Wheathampstead. They were unmoved. After Gaveston's death in 1312, he was buried at King's Langley, with the Abbot of St Albans, Hugh de Eversden, officiating.

After Edward's death in 1327, the Queen Mother, Isabella, 'She Wolf of France', lived at Berkhamsted and Hertford, where she died in 1358. King David of Scotland was held at Hertford after his capture in 1346.

Middle Ages

The Feudal system had placed every man in his station. The common man was tied to the land and owed his lord service for it, as his lord owed service to the king. He also had to attend his lord's court, use his lord's mill, and pay many sorts of duties and taxes to his lord.

The establishment of new towns meant that people had begun to break away from the land. By the thirteenth century we find that a tenant at Codicote could pay money to be 'quit of his works' for the lord. His duty was commuted to what is, in effect, rent. We also find another paying to absent himself from his manor.

The real breakdown of the feudal system, however, was caused by the Black Death, the plague which in 1348-9 'halved all flesh' according to a St Albans monk. We cannot know the death toll everywhere, but eighty-nine tenants died in Codicote alone. In sixty-eight parishes of the Diocese of Lincoln in Hertfordshire, twenty-seven new priests were instituted in 1349. There is a moving inscription recording the plague in Ashwell church tower. Translated from the Latin it reads:

'1350, wretched wild and distracted the dregs of the people survive to witness.' Another hand has added: 'The first plague was in 1339; at the end of the second a mighty wind this year, 1361, St Maurus thunders in heaven.'

The Black Death is usually stated to be the cause of the desertion of many villages. It is unlikely that the whole population of any village died. Many of the sixty or so deserted parishes in Hertfordshire were so small that the loss of a few people tipped the balance. The survivors moved to better land that had been vacated, or into other nearby villages. Labour became a valuable commodity, and landlords would now pay for services, and not ask where the labourer came from.

In many parts of England villages were deliberately depopulated to provide sheep grazing, which was less labour-intensive than arable farming. But, although several medieval wool merchants are known in the county and broadcloth and fulling mills are often referred to, it is likely that only one Hertfordshire village was turned into pasture – Cockernach, near Barkway, where the Prior of Royston was grazing 200 sheep in the fifteenth century.

Some villages were obliterated or moved by the local lord to make a park, and although only three Hertfordshire parks were listed in Domesday, by 1500 there were at least forty. One notable example of this emparkment was at Pendley, near Tring, where, between 1440 and 1461, Sir Robert Whittingham totally destroyed the village to make his park. It is one of the ironies of history that when the railway came in 1837, engineering problems meant that it missed Tring. The station, built to serve Tring, was named after the village of Pendley which had been 'cast down and laid to pasture' nearly 400 years earlier. At Tewin, emparkment did not take place until the eighteenth century, while at King's Langley a royal park was created without the destruction of the village. Here the manor was bought by Edward I in 1276, and in 1290 the deer park contained eight acres formerly meadow, and 120 formerly arable. In 1397 a further 160 acres of arable land was added. The maximum extent of the park was about 950 acres. After the Tudors abandoned Langley, it was recommended that it should 'be disparked'. Villages moved for other reasons, often to put themselves onto a main road so many Hertfordshire churches stand alone in the fields. The devil is often blamed!

The monks of St Albans were stricken by the Black Death. In 1349 the Abbot and more than three-quarters of the monks died but the Abbey survived, flourished, and had friends in high places. In 1356, after the capture of the French king, John, at Poitiers, the Black Prince entrusted Abbot de la Mare with the royal hostage.

The causes of the Peasants' Revolt in 1381 were both economic and social. As a result of the Black Death, many serfs had gained their freedom and were paid for their labour. Those who were not free rebelled. On the other hand, wages had been fixed by the Statute of Labourers while prices were not controlled. In Hertfordshire most of the peasants were free in fact if not in law, even if their pay was insufficient. The Abbey and its widespread estates were the focus of the revolt in the county, because the burghers in the Abbey markets of Barnet and St Albans who had most to gain.

Shortly after the rising in Kent the men of Barnet marched on St Albans, threatening to destroy the Abbey if the townsmen did not join them. The Abbot sent his servants with the rebel army as it marched south on London. At Mile End they met Richard II and Wat Tyler, leader of the revolt, and were given royal manumission (freedom). The mob returned, and the townsmen were freed by the Abbot. After more threats, the freedom was extended to the other Abbey manors: Abbots Langley, Watford, Hertford, Tring, Berkhamsted, Redbourn, Codicote, Shephall, Newnham, Aston, Northaw, Sandridge, Tyttenhanger, Cassiobury, Walden, Norton and Hexton. After the death of Wat Tyler and Jack Straw the revolt was crushed. Eighteen of the leaders of the Hertfordshire revolt were hanged and drawn and many imprisoned for 'seizing royal powers'. Nothing had changed but there were many instances of arson against Abbey property and other confrontations over the years.

Geoffrey Chaucer, author of *Canterbury Tales*, was Clerk of Works of the Royal Castle at Berkhamsted in a post held by Thomas à Beckett two centuries before, and Richard II often kept court at Langley, where he was buried after lying in state at the Abbey. Henry Bolingbroke held court at Hertford after landing in 1399 and Edmund, Duke of York, his uncle, called a council at St Albans to discuss defence – but his cousin, Richard II was forced to abdicate. Edmund

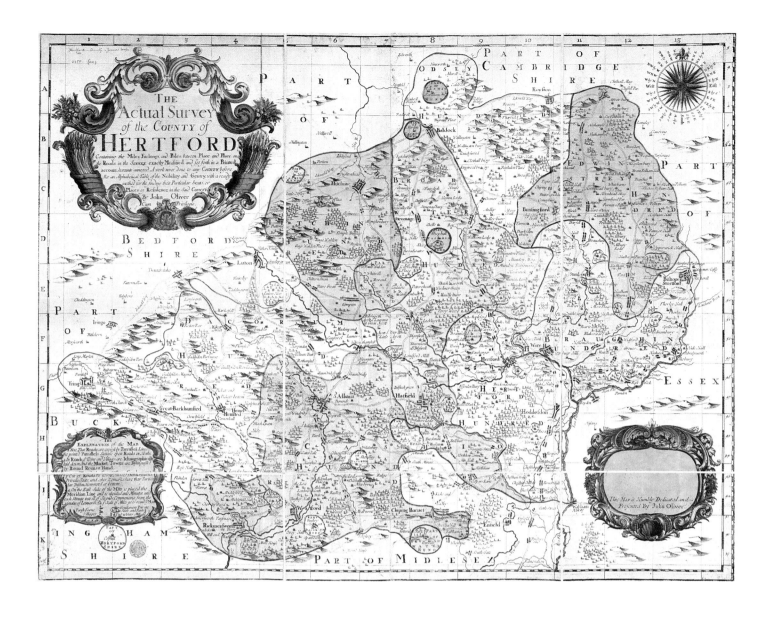

was buried at Langley in 1402.

Henry V kept Easter 1413 at Langley and Queen Catherine held Hertford Castle, which had become the traditional possession of royal wives. Sir John Mortimer of Hatfield was executed after Oldcastle's conspiracy against Henry V in 1421. Edmund Tudor, father of Henry VII, was born at Hadham, where Owen Tudor and Catherine, Henry V's widow, 'lived as man and wife,' according to later accounts by followers of Richard III, who thus hinted at Tudor bastardy.

Abbot Whethamstede of St Albans praised Henry VI as a simple, upright man, easily led into unwise decisions and prodigality. He was also bankrupt, with his administration under attack from all sides. Richard of York, descendant of Edmund of Langley, landed from exile in Ireland in 1450, determined to intervene. He was confronted 'beyond Sent Albons' by Sir Thomas Hoo, but marched on London, hoping to push an Act of Resumption through Parliament to cancel Henry's lavish grants to his favourites. That failed, and he attempted a *coup d'état*, which also failed. He retired in disgrace to Ludlow, only to emerge as Protector of England when the king became insane in 1454. His supporters included Warwick, whom later generations called the *Kingmaker*, while his enemies, the Lancastrians and their associates, included the Queen, Margaret of Anjou mother of the new-born Edward, Prince of Wales.

Three battles of the Wars of the Roses were fought in Hertfordshire, including the first, in 1455. Two took place in St Albans. You can stand in the market place in St Peter's Street and imagine, during the first engagement, the crashing of the battering rams as the Yorkist army broke through the houses, close to where, centuries later, Telford broke through with his new London Road. Or you can look up to the top of the clocktower and imagine the Yorkist archers showering arrows down on the Lancastrians advancing up George Street in 1461. On Barnet Common is a monument where, in a confused encounter on a misty morning in 1471, Warwick was slain.

In 1483 Buckingham, Constable of England, who held Hoddesdon and Hertford, rose to support the expected landing of Henry Tudor, and was later executed. Richard III's court was at Berkhamsted, and it was from here he went to Bosworth and his death in 1485.

The Devil and All His Works

The devil has always been active in Hertfordshire. His thunderbolts and toenails are common fossils of the boulder clay, and his special plants flourish in the fields. He is a great digger and delver and is blamed for many mounds and holes. He haunts the sunken ways and created Devil's Ditch near Gorhambury, Devil's Dyke at Wheathampstead and Grim's Ditch near Tring, which he dug for Sir Guy de Gravade the alchemist, who bartered his soul for knowledge of alchemy and necromancy. But he miscalculated in a dispute with his servant, John Bond, called upon the devil for aid and disappeared in a clap of thunder, along with his castle and all it contained. The devil dug the moat in Whomerly Wood, Stevenage, and threw the earth at Gravely church, knocking the steeple off and forming the steep hill beside the churchyard. The soil that fell short formed the Six Hills beside the Great North Road.

It seems that the devil kept knocking steeples off, which is why the majority of the county's churches have a tower topped with a small 'Hertfordshire spike'. He was also so strong in these parts that he dictated the peculiar location of many of the churches, including St Paul's Walden, Stanstead Abbots, Pirton, and Walkern.

In 1086 one Piers Shonks was buried half-way through the wall of Brent Pelham church since the devil had sworn to have him whether he was buried inside the church or out, as a punishment for killing the last dragon in England. It can be seen carved on the top of Shonks's tomb. Nearby, a blind fiddler wagered in a pub that he would explore the Anstey Cave, said to contain the devil, while his mates followed the sound of his fiddle safely in the fields above. The music stopped, and George was never seen again. His little dog came home alone, with all its hair and its tail burnt off as if by a blowlamp.

At Long Marston the Boot Inn commemorates Sir John Shorne, rector, who, about 1300, conjured the devil into his boot making North Marston a place of pilgrimage where the votaries could take the waters at St John's spring, and buy, as a souvenir, the first Jack-in-the-box.

In 1648 a pamphlet was printed, 'Attested by divers Letters of Men of very good Credit in the Town,' which records how the devil appeared in a St Albans cellar in the form of a ram, which a local butcher killed, selling some of the meat and serving the rest for supper for a large number of guests. In 1678 another fly-sheet, with a picture, tells how a farmer, saying that the mower asked too much to harvest his oats, 'swore *That ther Devil should mow it rather than He*. And so it fell out, that very night the Crop of Oat shew'd as if it had been all of a Flame, but next Morning appear'd so neatly mow'd by the Devil or some Infernal Spirit, that no Mortal Man was able to do the like. And how the Oats ly now in the Field, and the Owner has not the Power to fetch them away.'

Soothsayers and necromancers changed the course of history in the Wars of the Roses. A Lancastrian Duke, warned to shun castles, died on the steps of the Castle Inn in the first Battle of St Albans, in 1455 – 'underneath an alehouse paltry sign, The Castle of St Albans, Somerset Hath made the wizard famous in his death,' wrote Shakespeare 130 years later. During the battle of Barnet at Easter 1471 Friar Bungay, who travelled with the Yorkist army, conjured up a thick mist. Warwick's men, mistaking the star badge worn by de Vere's followers for the rose and sun of Edward IV, fought their allies, and lost the battle.

Before the National Health service, almost every parish had its wizard or witch, a person with special knowledge often used to cure or alleviate sickness. It was said of them that they could fly on broomsticks or hurdles, and change themselves into animals. They often maintained themselves and protected their secrets with the threat of their magic, like Sally Rainbow, who lived in a cave at Bramfield. The local farmers gave her anything she asked, lest she overlooked their cattle and infected them, and she provided a safe refuge for Dick Turpin. Others profited by protecting the common people from the witches. Dr William Drage of Hitchin (1637-68) wrote a treatise on *Diseases from Witchcraft*, which he cured by 'suffumigation and ceremonies'. He witnessed many 'examinations' of witches by the Catch-22 method of tying their thumbs together and throwing them into the nearest pond or stream. If they floated they were guilty, and burned. If they sank they were not guilty, and drowned.

Until the eighteenth century an accusation of witchcraft was a way of removing someone feared, disliked or envied. The last witch tried and found guilty in England was Jane Wenham of Walkern who was brought to trial by Sir Henry Chauncy, Recorder of Hertford – who incidentally was the first published historian of the county, and great nephew of the Vicar of Ware who became President of Harvard College. She was found guilty in 1711, but pardoned and lived under the protection of the local squire until 1730. Her case promoted a great outcry and led to the Witchcraft Act of 1736 which stopped prosecution. Despite this, two elderly people, Ruth and John Osborne, were drowned in 1751 as a result of a public ducking at Tring. The ringleader, Thomas Colley, a chimney sweep, was hanged and gibbetted at Gubblecote, and is said to haunt the site as a giant black dog.

The Tudor Period

Henry Tudor was the son of Edmund Tudor, born at Hadham to Catherine, Widow of Henry V. His claim to the throne may have been weak but his administration was strong. His chief adviser was Cardinal Morton, who invented 'Morton's Fork', the catch-all method of taxation. If you made a display of wealth you could afford to make a large voluntary contribution to the royal coffers, whereas if you lived a less ostentatious life you must be making economies so that you could also make large voluntary contributions . . . In 1480-90 Morton built the first brick palace at Hatfield which became important in later years as a royal palace.

Henry VIII was no stranger to the county. As a young prince, before he put on weight, he was nearly drowned in a ditch at Wymondley when his vaulting pole snapped. As King he stayed at Hertford castle with Catherine his wife and Anne Boleyn his mistress. In 1528, they caught 'sweating sickness'. While the King and Queen retired to Hunsdon, which the King had bought from the Boleyn family and rebuilt in brick, Anne was sent back to Kent.

Later, during the divorce proceedings, Catherine stayed at The More (Moore Park) in a fifteenth-century brick

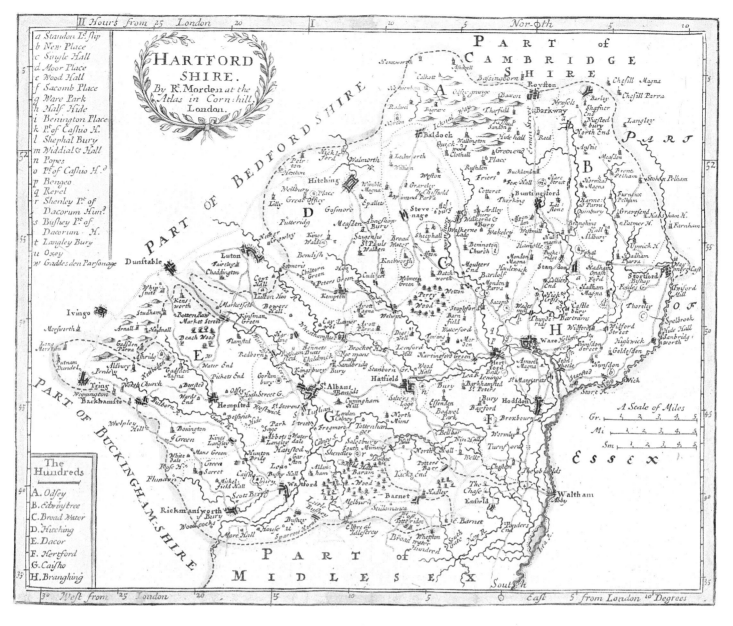

'Hartford Shire' by Robert Morden, 1701

Robert Morden was a map and bookseller and maker of instruments and globes who operated from premises in New Cheapside and Cornhill. His shop, as can be seen from the map, was called (appropriately) The Atlas. Morden is perhaps best known for his sets of playing cards showing county maps which are very popular with collectors today and fetch high prices. His maps, which appeared in Camden's Britannia, *a popular history of Britain in the seventeenth century, were based on other mapmakers' work and have been criticised as inaccurate. But Morden's style of mapmaking was clear and unfussy, allowing roads to be seen, and with more modern spelling of the placenames represented an advance in county mapping. He never claimed to have made a proper survey and his maps were only intended to complement a history book 'carrying the eye of the reader from place to place as he peruses the text.'*
(By courtesy of Valerie Scott)

Many people did not attend church, but 'resorte unto Alehouses, and theyre exercyseth unlawful games with greate swearying, blasphyme and drunkennes and other enormyties'.

When the dissolution came, there was little opposition. Some houses, such as St Mary de Pré, were empty and some heads of houses, such as Bishop Borman at St Albans (who had been imprisoned for debt), were given golden handshakes while others, as for instance Prior Ingworth at Langley, were given large pensions.

By 1540, largely as a result of confiscation of the estates of the religious houses, especially those of St Albans, one-third of the county was in the King's hands. However, during the next ten years most of this had been disposed of and mainly because the buyers were businessmen rather than courtiers or noblemen, successive owners bought and sold estates without concern for establishing hereditary title. The seeds of the later political independence of the county were sown early.

Roads are not marked on the earliest maps, but road books or itineraries were produced from the middle of the fifteenth century. The first main road listed – the A1 of its day – had been the pilgrims' route, Palmers' Way, between Walsingham and London. Part of this ran along Ermine Street, now a track parallel to the A10, and it is difficult today to imagine the road from Braughing to Barley as having been part of the principal road in England.

house, erected by the Archbishop of York, which then belonged to Cardinal Wolsey. Henry was at Tyttenhanger when, according to tradition, he married Anne secretly at Sopwell.

The Church at this time seems to have been in a disgraceful state. Many of the clergy were absentee, leaving curates to officiate, and many held more than one living. The fabric of the buildings was often described as ruinous.

Henry VIII's children spent much of their early lives in the county. Mary, declared illegitimate, was maid-in-waiting to her sister Elizabeth at Hatfield Palace, which Henry had kept after the Dissolution. After the death of Anne, when both the girls became illegitimate, they moved to Hunsdon where their legitimacy became irrelevant with the birth of an heir apparent, Edward, whose christening they both attended in 1537. Edward spent most of his youth at Ashridge, another royal estate remaining from confiscated monastic lands, but he was at Hatfield when he became Edward VI on the death of his father in 1547.

During Edward's reign Elizabeth resided either at Cheshunt, in a house that belonged to Cardinal Wolsey, or at Hatfield, while Mary made her home at Hunsdon. On the death of Edward in 1553 Mary fled to Norfolk and Elizabeth stayed put. After Mary's coronation Elizabeth rode north to Ashridge with 500 gentlemen in green and white livery – almost a private army – but was sent to the Tower after the Wyat rebellion against Mary in 1554, and many Hertfordshire men were placed under house arrest. Wyat however, refused to compromise Elizabeth, even to save his own neck, and she was released.

On 17th November, 1558, Elizabeth was sitting under an oak tree at Hatfield when she was brought the news of Mary's death and her own accession. Her first Privy Council was held in the Great Hall there and William Cecil was appointed her Secretary of State.

During her reign Elizabeth was a frequent visitor to Hertfordshire and, during plagues in London in 1561 and 1581, her parliament met in Hertford. She visited Henry Carey, now Lord Hunsdon, and her more illustrious courtiers, such as William Cecil, who, created Lord Burghley in 1571, built a great house at Theobalds. Sir Nicholas Bacon, Lord Chancellor, extended his house at Gorhambury to accommodate her entourage. 'My lord,' she is reported to have said at her first visit, 'what a small house you have gotten.' 'Madam,' he replied, 'my house is well, but you have made me too great for my house!' The additions for her next visit included a gallery 120 feet long and when a courtier undiplomatically referred to Sir Nicholas as 'a gross man', Elizabeth corrected him with 'Sir Nicholas's soul is well-housed'.

Only the great hall of Elizabeth's (and Cardinal Morton's) Hatfield Palace remains beside the Jacobean house that replaced it. Theobalds was totally demolished by the Commonwealth and of Bacon's Gorhambury only the porch and fragments of the hall remain standing near its late-eighteenth-century replacement.

Hertfordshire was particularly proud of the part its men played in Elizabeth's campaigns, both abroad and in mobilisation against the Armada.

Jacobean Influence

As Elizabeth's funeral was taking place in March 1603, James I, son of her enemy Mary, was being feasted at Royston on his way south from Scotland to be crowned. He liked Royston so much that he rented Robert Chester's house at

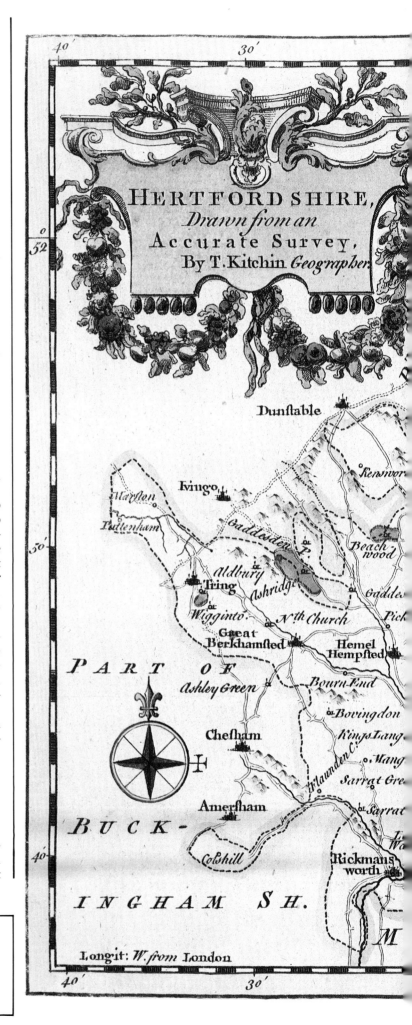

'Hertfordshire' by Thomas Kitchin, 1748
This map of the county appeared in the London Magazine. *It was engraved by Thomas Kitchin (died 1784) who worked from an address in Holborn as an engraver and publisher. Kitchin's maps are reasonably priced and a good starting point for county collectors on a tight budget.* (By courtesy of Valerie Scott)

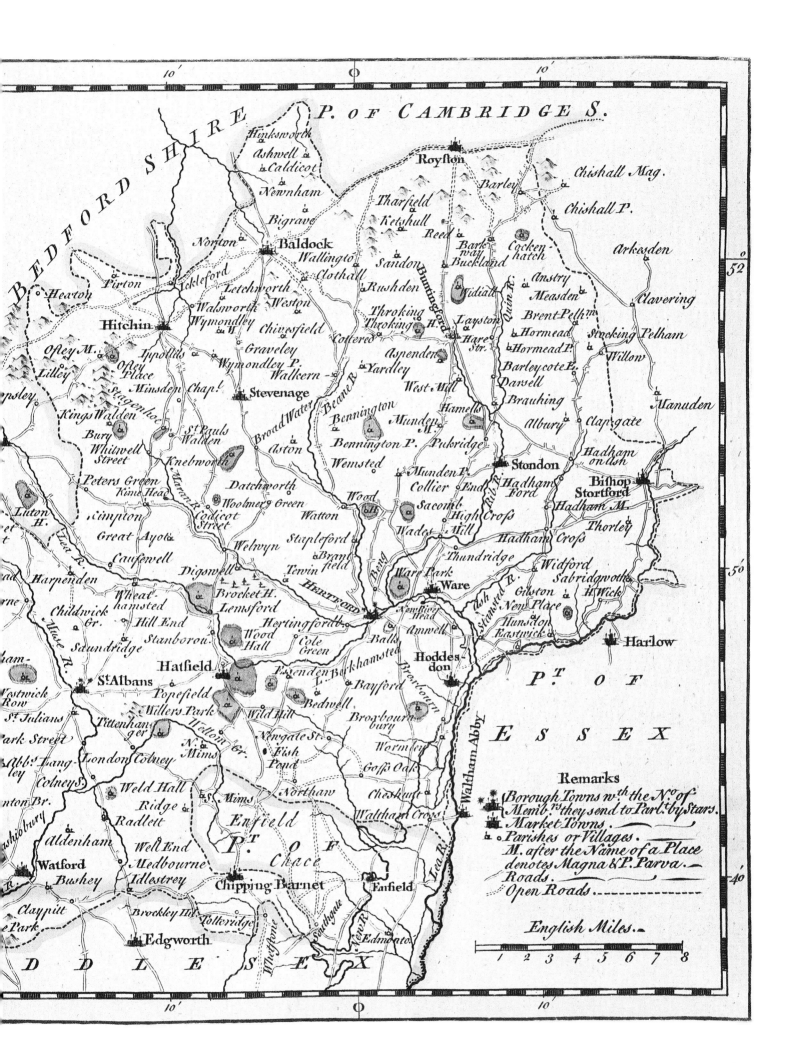

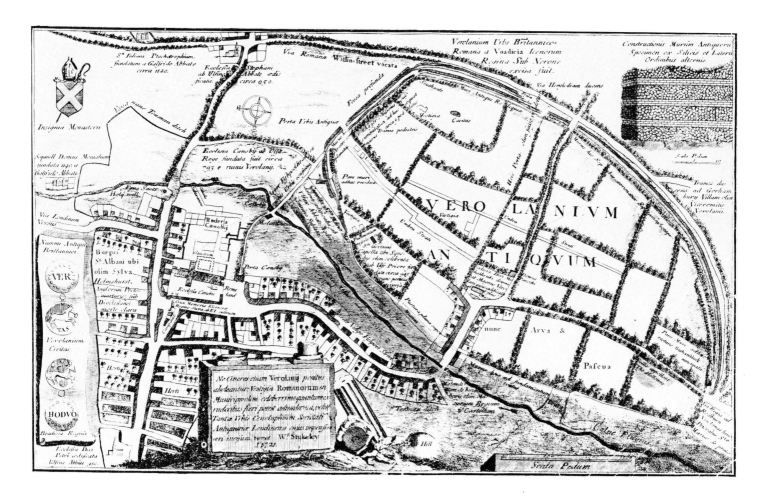

the Priory while the Cock and Greyhound Inn was converted into a royal hunting lodge in which he spent much of his reign. So that he could ride in comfort and safety, fences were taken down, ridge and furrow ploughing stopped, pigs had rings put in their noses to prevent them rooting holes, roads and bridges were kept under repair, and 'persons of base condition and scholars from Cambridge' were kept away.

But this kind of hospitality palled after a while and one day James I's favourite dog, Jowler, came home with a message on his collar: 'Good Mr Jowler, we pray you speak to the King (for he hears you every day and he doth not us) that it will please his Majesty to go back to London, for else the country (county) will be undone; all our provision is spent already and we cannot entertain him longer.'

James admired Cecil's great house at Theobalds and insisted that it should be swapped for the old brick palace at Hatfield. Cecil built the present Jacobean house, arguably the most important in England, and demolished all but the hall of its predecessor. Theobalds was made even larger and a nine-mile wall built round the park. Charles I was brought up there, and James I died there. The royal castles, however, became disused and were demolished. The same fate befell the Royal palace at King's Langley, where the park was returned to agriculture in 1627.

Francis Bacon, son of Elizabeth's Chancellor, Sir Nicholas, became Chancellor to James I. It was said that when he was at Gorhambury it seemed that the court must be there, so rich was his household. He was eventually disgraced for corruption but is remembered today for his essays and his philosophical works for which he was called the father of the scientific method.

In the years following the death of Henry VIII, the church was in turmoil, with bewildered churchwardens moving furniture and fittings, shrines and 'monuments to superstition' in and out, priests being sworn, foresworn and dismissed. Under Mary, heretics were burned: William Hale at Barnet, Thomas Fust at Ware, and George Tankerville at St Albans. Under Elizabeth, several priests were dismissed for 'adherence to the old learning', although it seemed the word 'learning', might have been misused. In the Deanery of Braughing, for instance, of twenty-nine clergy, only nine were graduates, eleven had a 'slight to middling knowledge of Latin, three had no Latin, and eighteen had a slight to middling knowledge of Theology'. No wonder there was protest.

In 1573, John Field became Curate of Bovingdon after release from prison where he had languished for admonishing Parliament that ministers should be elected by their congregations. He was a friend of the Bacons at Gorhambury, whose parish priest, William Dyke, was said to be 'troubling his auditory with new opinions and notions, thwarting the established religion'.

Many left Hertfordshire to seek the New World in the seventeenth century, among them Charles Chauncy, vicar of Ware, later to become the first President of Harvard College and William Denison from Bishop's Stortford who in 1631 took with him a stepson, Daniel Monk, who rose to become Overseer of Harvard as well as Town Clerk, Commander of the New England Militia, and Speaker of the General Court of the Colony (two of Denison's daughters married men who also became Presidents of Harvard). John Eliot from Widford was the first to preach to the Indians in their own tongue in 1643, and his Catechism was the first printed book in their language. The ancestors of the American poet Ralph Waldo Emerson left Bishop's Stortford in 1638.

When both James I, and later his son Charles I, claimed a divine right to tax the people without consent, protestantism became a political issue. Neighbours, even members of the same family, found themselves on opposite sides when civil war broke out in 1642.

As in previous conflicts, Hertfordshire suffered greatly from its geographical position, as armies camped in the county or stopped in transit. St Albans, home of one Colonel Cox, a friend of Cromwell, was often used as a headquarters by the Earl of Essex, who lived at Cassiobury. Two thousand men were accommodated on their way to Edgehill in October 1642. Later the town was garrisoned and strengthened while Lady Sussex, at Gorhambury, was given special protection – one supposes from the soldiers.

There were numerous reports of violence against persons and property by both sides throughout the county. One of the worst periods was the winter of 1643-4 when a mutinous, unpaid and ill-fed parliamentary army stayed at St Albans. In 1645, before Naseby, twelve men were tried at St Albans for various offences and two of them were executed. After Naseby when the Roundhead army and their prisoners were billeted at Redbourn and St Albans, windows were taken from the churches, which were used as accommodation, to ventilate them.

In 1647 the war should have been over, but Parliament could not demobilise the Model Army, which it had decreed should not be brought within twenty-five miles of the capital. Camped on Thriploe Heath, Royston, the army held its own parliament and wrote to London, demanding a purge of the House and pay for the troops. After marching on St Albans, they were sent one month's pay for 20,000 men. They held off London, and the incident where the 'Levellers' demanded democracy for the army took place at Cockbush (or Corkbush) field, Ware. The County complained to Parliament about having to provide quarters and provisions.

Following prayers and a meeting in the Abbey at St Albans, Ireton's 'remonstrance', demanding the trial of the King, was sent in 1648. Crop failure was making provisioning the army almost impossible, but the county was saved when the army moved north to Scotland following the execution of Charles I.

For a time, Oliver Cromwell's son, Richard, lived at Theobalds, but under the Commonwealth there was no more religious toleration than before. High church priests replaced, Baptists were imprisoned, and many, mostly Quakers, punished for non-payment of tithes: ninety-four went to prison in 1660.

The Restoration meant another round of musical chairs both civil and ecclesiastic. Property which had been confiscated was restored and posts refilled. Forty parsons were dismissed, many becoming 'public preachers', and in 1661 twenty-two Quakers went to prison in Hertford. Some were sentenced to transportation, but the ships' masters refused to take them. At this time Bunyan preached in the county. Many nonconformist chapels were built after the Declaration of Indulgence in 1672, but the oldest Quaker Meeting House still in use in England today was built in Hertford in 1672.

The nomination of Charles II's brother James, a Catholic, as his heir, led to a plot to assassinate them both near Rye House in 1683. The plot was betrayed, and was used as an excuse for a purge of all Whig leaders. In 1685 several Hertfordshire men were implicated in the rebellion which sought to put his bastard son, the Duke of Monmouth, on the throne. County Justices were instructed to 'search suspicious places and houses for any of the rebels of

'A Map of Hertfordshire . . .' by George Bickham, c.1754

There has been some controversy as to whether or not this panoramic view of the county constitutes a map. It would certainly have been very difficult to use as a routefinder but gives a good flavour of the area in the eighteenth century – an attractive bird's eye view. The 'map' appeared in a work by George Bickham entitled The British Monarchy : or, a new chorographical description of all the dominions subject to the King of Great Britain *. . . . and is dedicated to the Earl of Essex, Lord Lieutenant of the county. The rivers and main towns are named. (By courtesy of the British Library)*

their abettors'.

Lawrence Hyde, Earl of Rochester and Lord Lieutenant of Hertfordshire, was one of the seven signatories of the petition which brought William of Orange to the throne in 1689, but it was John Somers, scholar, linguist and barrister, who persuaded Parliament that James II had abdicated and made the way easy for William. He lived at North Mimms and was first adviser, then Chancellor to William, framed the Declaration of Rights, a second Magna Carta, and was instrumental in the Union with Scotland. He died Baron Somers of Evesham in 1716.

Highways and highwaymen

In 1555, by coincidence the year of the building of the first English coach, an Act of Parliament had made the parishes responsible for the maintenance of their own roads. After the Roman period, a few roads had been maintained by interested parties – monasteries, palaces and markets – but few long journeys were made and most roads were unsuitable for wheeled vehicles. Now all the men of the parish had to give four, later six, days' work per year on the roads, supplying both materials and tools. For small parishes on main roads the task was impossible, and if on clay (with no stones for repairing roads), doubly so, as at Radwell on the North Road, perhaps the inspiration for the Slough of Despond in John Bunyan's *Pilgrim's Progress:* 'This miry slough is such a place as cannot be mended.'

It was to maintain this very road that, in 1663, after more than half a century of debate, the first 'Turnpike' Act enabled the Justices to levy tolls from travellers. The scheme was adopted in other places, and in the eighteenth century Turnpike Trusts were appointed to operate it. There were fifteen trusts in Hertfordshire, maintaining main roads which were mostly radial from London, except for one, from Hatfield through Watford – the 'Gout Track', said to have been constructed to allow the Earls of Salisbury and Essex to travel in comfort to Bath from Hatfield and Cassiobury.

With so many main roads passing through, there are not surprisingly a great number of stories about highwaymen in Hertfordshire. Dick Turpin's name comes up all along the Great North Road, especially near Welwyn, despite the fact that there is no evidence that he ever used it. The famous ride to York in a day, if it ever took place, was by another highwayman, 'Swift Nicks', sixty years earlier from Gad's Hill (near Gravesend) via Chelmsford and Cambridge. Nevertheless we are told where he hid his spoils at Robbery Bottom, a dark sunken place north of Welwyn, also associated with 'Captain' Witney and 'Redbeard' (a Hertfordshire pronunciation? It's by *Rably* Heath!), we can see the chair he sat on at The Red Lion, and where he hid, with the witch, Sally Rainbow, in a cave at Bramfield.

Probably the most romantic legend concerns Katherine Ferrers, 'The Wicked Lady' who dressed as a man to rob travellers during the Civil War. Sir Knighton Ferrers, her father, died before she was born, and her mother married a Royalist, Sir Simon Fanshawe of Ware Park. With her mother she was a refugee from the Parliamentarians in Huntingdonshire until, aged twelve, she was an unwilling bride to Fanshawe's son. At eighteen she returned to her family home, Markyate Cell, and joined Ralph Chaplin, a local farmer who preyed upon travellers on the nearby Watling Street. After he was shot during a robbery on Finchley Common she started a reign of terror against persons and property until she herself was shot on Nomansland Common, returning, dying, to a secret room at Markyate Cell, which she is still said to haunt today.

A less romantic man was leader of a gang that robbed and killed people returning from Hertford Market. Late on December 28, 1782, the gang tried to stop Farmer Whittenbury, who prudently fled to Queen Hoo to summons help. In the resulting fight the leader was shot. He was Walter Clibborn, who sold pies in the market while selecting potential victims, and is buried by the side of the road where he died, with a stake through his heart.

Perhaps the best example of private enterprise recorded is that of Joshua Cass, who, in 1675, erected and maintained his own 'turn picke' on the bridge at Amwell, collecting tolls from unsuspecting travellers and putting the money into his own pocket.

Eighteenth Century

In 1724 Daniel Defoe wrote of Hertfordshire in his *Tour through the Whole Island of Great Britain:*

'The County is under several characters. The part of it adjoining Bedfordshire is Whiggish and full of dissenters. That part of it adjoining to Huntingdonshire, Cam-

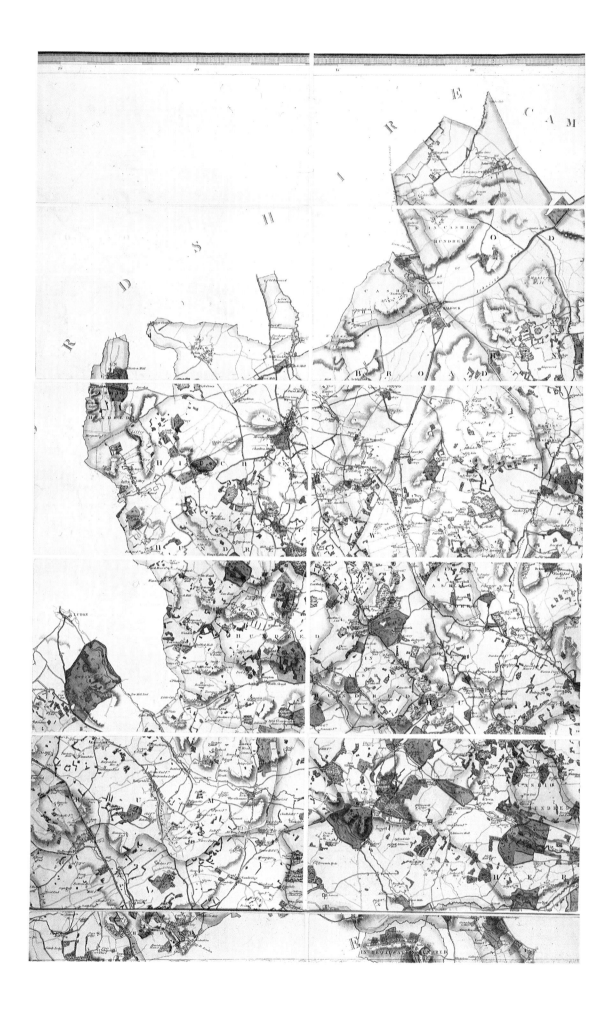

bridgeshire and Essex entirely Church and of the High Sort.'

The Justices, outspoken in the interests of political stability, sent loyal addresses to William III and to Queen Anne, but suddenly seem to have become more concerned with domestic affairs after the accession of George I. There were demonstrations in favour of James Stuart, and Oakapple Day, commemorating the Restoration, was celebrated at St Michael's until the last century by a fair, decorated with oak boughs.

At this time two Members of Parliament were returned by each of the boroughs, St Albans and Hertford, and two by the County. Borough elections in the eighteenth and nineteenth centuries were so corrupt that petitions were often made against the results – usually successfully. It was reported that bribes at St Albans were not paid until after the last possible date for challenge! Thomas Oldfield, author of *A Complete History, Personal and Political, of the Boroughs of Great Britain . . .* records, unemotionally, of Hertford in 1794: 'Baron Dimsdale possesses the principle interest in the Borough, and can secure the election of one member. The other is usually contested.' Of St Albans: 'The influence in this borough is divided between Earl Spencer and Lord Grimston, each of whom returns one Member of Parliament.' The Spencer interest was inherited by Sarah, Lady Churchill, who was born Sarah Jennings in 1660 at Water End near Wheathampstead. In 1678 she married John Churchill, who was created Duke of Marlborough in 1702, and lived at Holywell House, St Albans, until the completion of Blenheim Palace. Blenheim was a gift to her husband, the greatest general of his time, from Queen Anne, and birthplace of her great statesman descendent, Winston Churchill.

The county (as opposed to the boroughs) was noted for its independence because most of the landowners, who were the electorate, were self-made men unaffected by hereditary tradition.

Many houses were either rebuilt entirely or else cased in brickwork in the eighteenth century, and many parks were landscaped. Notable was Moor Park, where Benjamin Styles, who made a fortune from the South Sea Bubble, spent £130,000 on improvements to his newly acquired house. He even had part of a hill removed to improve the view. Alexander Pope wrote:

'Or cut wide views through mountains to the plain, You'll wish your hill a sheltered seat again.'

The works of Capability Brown and Repton have left their mark throughout the county. Arthur Young wrote, in 1804:

'Property in Hertfordshire is much divided: the vicinity

'Hertfordshire' by Thomas Moule c.1842
This pretty map is decorated with vignettes of St. Albans Abbey and Cassiobury House in Watford which was the home of the Earls of Essex for over 250 years until its demolition in 1927. Moule's maps are much sought after by collectors because they are a good size for framing and not too expensive. Moule, who was a heraldry expert and worked in the General Post Office, first produced his maps in parts. They were later put together in his work The English Counties Delineated : or a Topographical Description of England : Illustrated by a complete series of county maps *by Thomas Moule. Moule's first maps did not show railways but the one shown here obviously comes from a later edition as the London to Birmingham railway appears. (By courtesy of Map House)*

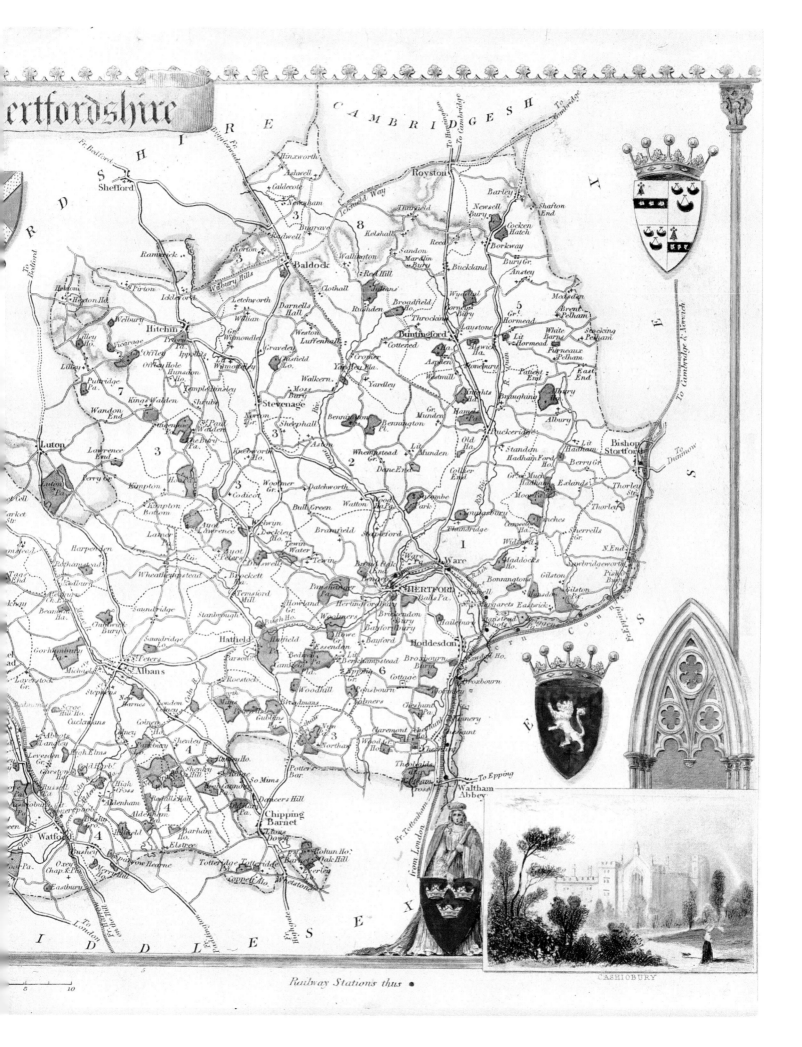

ertfordshire

CAMBRIDGESH

Railway Stations thus ●

CASHIOBURY

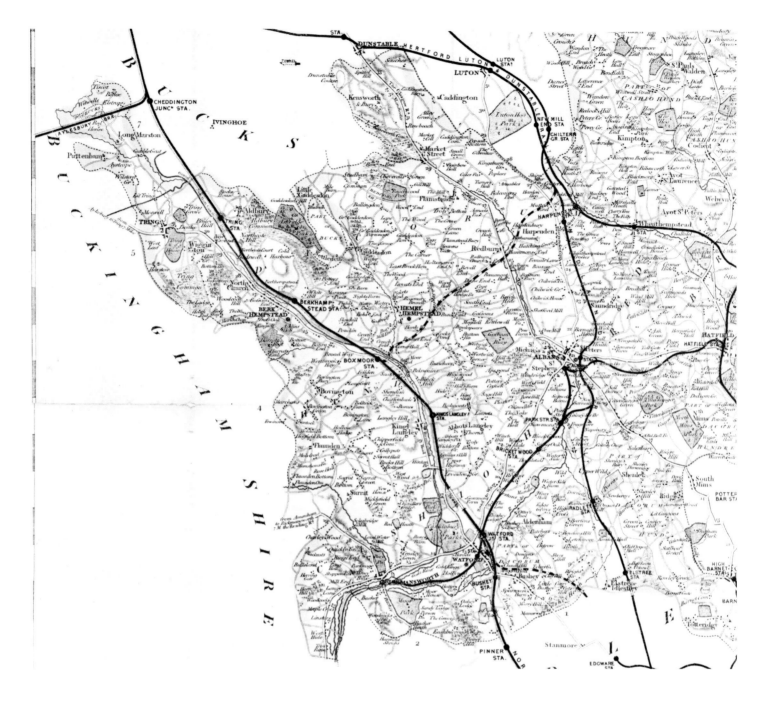

'Cruchley's Road and Railway Map of the County of Hertford' c.1883

The coming of the railway totally changed the lives of people in Hertfordshire. It made it possible to send fresh produce to the London market from almost anywhere in the county; it brought ideas and products of the industrial revolution and enabled people to make journeys hitherto unimaginable. Above all it made commuting to London possible. This section of Cruchley's road and railway map shows the extensive network of railways in the late nineteenth century. There was even a branch line from Cheddington village to Aylesbury. G.F. Cruchley was a mapseller and globe maker who worked from an address in Fleet Street, London. All his railway maps are lithographic reproductions of maps engraved earlier by John Cary. (By courtesy of the British Library)

sons to purchase land for building villas: this has multiplied estates in a manner unknown in more distant counties. A considerable addition is made to the beauty of this county, by the villas and seats of the rich proprietors presenting themselves to view in every direction. Although they occupy a considerable space of ground, which would otherwise be held by common farmers: yet their decorated lawns, and ornamental grounds, not only adorn the country, and please the traveller's eye by their neatness and general beauty, but also may be considered as a national benefit from the very extensive employment they supply the industrious poor in their neighbourhood.'

In *The Agreeable Historian,* Simpson had summed up the rest when he wrote, in 1745:

'As there is little or no manufacture in the Shire, which is full of Maltsers, Millers, Dealers in Corn & C., so the trade would be inconsiderable, were it not for its being every Way a great Thorough-fare, and for its neighbourhood to *London,* which makes the chief Market-Towns to be much frequented for the sale of Wheat and Barley,

of the capital, the goodness of the air and the roads and the beauty of the country have much contributed to this circumstance, by making this county a favourite residence and by attracting great numbers of wealthy per-

and all sorts of Grain, not only the growth of this but of several other Shires.'

Turnpike trusts improved the thoroughfares; people were moving into service industries in the expanding towns along them; there was employment on the country estates, and agriculture was improving as everywhere in the country. The land, with the exception of the north-east on the borders of Cambridgeshire, was mostly enclosed and the mid 1800's was the golden age of the corn dealer in the county. London began to outbid the local markets; a profitable scarcity almost turned to famine. There were bread and wage riots, and outbreaks of incendiarism. The words of Walker in 1795 give an epitaph for the century:

> The scanty allowance of a parish to alleviate the wants of starving children is a poor compensation to an honest hard-working father for the loss of that labour by which he had cheerfully sustained them.

Air and Water

Waterways can carry very large loads with little effort or wear and tear. This fact was certainly appreciated by the Romans and even when they no longer kept the smaller rivers open to navigation, the Lea could still be used, as witness the incursion of the Danes in the ninth century.

The potential of the river to carry produce, especially malt, from the rich north-east of the county to London, is well recorded. In 1220 Margaret, Countess of Winchester granted the Canons of Holy Trinity passage for corn from Ware to London. In 1300 the people of Ware blocked the river to traffic from Hertford and in 1355 a commission was appointed to remove such 'annoyances'.

Other commissions repaired and inspected weirs and sluices, and were authorised to collect tolls. Boatmen competed with carters, who tried to sabotage the waterway, and also with millers:

> 'The head of the Abbot of Waltham's Myll where water goeth out of the Kynges Streame is of xvj foote broade where it should be but fower foote by which the Kynges Streame is so hurt . . .' (1482).

In 1571 an Act 'for bryngynge of ye River Lee to ye northside of Ye Citie of London' entailed a four mile cut to Moorgate. In 1580 the first pound lock was built at Waltham:

> 'A rare devise see but newly made a Waterworke the locke through which the Boates of Ware doe passe with Malt. This locke contains two double doors of woode, within the cisterne all of plankes which only fills when boates come there to passe by opening these mighty doores by sleight.'

In the second half of the eighteenth century, the Lea-Stort Navigation improved the Lea and its eastern tributary in emulation of the new canals being built elsewhere. At this time 1250 tons of malt were taken to London each week, and the return journey carried loads of refuse and manure to spread on the fields.

A canal runs down the Lea valley, not for navigation, but to supply fresh water to the capital. Called 'The New River', it was engineered from Amwell to Stoke Newington by Sir Hugh Middleton in 1609. Since Amwell spring failed in the nineteenth century, water has been taken from the Lea just downstream from Hertford.

Although at the end of the eighteenth century it was possible to send goods by canal to London from Birmingham through Oxford and the Thames, the journey was 248 miles long and needed 109 locks. In 1793 an Act enabled a new canal, the Grand Junction, to be built. It joined Brentford to Braunstone, just over ninety miles, using 121 locks but shortening the journey to Birmingham by 123 miles. Twenty miles of the canal were constructed in Hertfordshire, using the Gade valley route through the Chilterns. The Earls of Essex and Clarendon allowed it through their parks at Cassiobury and Grove Park only if designed as a landscape feature.

Work reached the summit at Tring, 382 feet above sea level, in 1799, and a through route was opened (partly by horse railway) in 1800. Supplying water at the top, on chalk, was a great problem because each barge took 100,000 gallons of water with it down each side. Reservoirs, wells and pumping houses had to be constructed in the north of the county and over the border. The Grand Junction (later Grand Union) Canal was the first major transport link between the capital and the industrial Midlands and even after the railways came, traffic rose to a maximum of about 1.4 million tons in 1868.

Hard times

Church houses were first built in the fifteenth century to accommodate the more secular functions of the parish. They took on the duties of taverns and accommodation for the sick and poor. By the end of the sixteenth century they provided work (and training) for paupers. At St Albans in 1618 the skills of weaving 'curious woollens and excellent yarns' were taught, and at Hitchin, in 1630, 'the mystery of flax dressing, the spinning of line and the making of straw hats'. At Langley, in 1753 the churchwardens:

> 'Shall Indever to inquier into the afares of the Church Houses in order to Make a Work Hous of them for the maintaince of the poor and to see that they are took Care of to be in ploied an ceep in a desan manner . . .'

Under the Workhouse Act of 1723, forty-eight Hertfordshire parishes provided workhouses, but their philosophy was in effect that poverty was a crime. In 1795 the Justices recommended that landed proprietors should give a 'poor rate' to their parishes. Under this arrangement the poor were let to a master who was expected to keep them and actually make a profit from their work. In fact most of them were either very young, very old, or infirm and profitable employment was seldom found for them. At Royston, boys and girls were apparently sold to a cotton master at Warrington. The overseer enquiried: 'What sum you will give with each and whether besides you will be at the expense of their respective journeys . . . ?'

A Poor Law Commission's report of 1833 brought quick response. At Hadham:

> 'Task and piece work shall be provided . . . Those who under plea of sickness or bodily infirmity refuse to gain livelyhood on these terms shall be received at once into the workhouse . . . All . . . shall surrender all their goods, clothing, property to the parish officers.'

Sexes were segregated, men's hair was cut close to the head like convicts', uniform had to be worn (at Hitchin with letters 'HU' in red paint four inches high), smoking and spirits were forbidden, doors had to be kept closed and inmates were not allowed to communicate with outsiders.

'Unions', workhouses for groups of parishes, were set up in 1847; apart from 'casuals' – tramps doing work for a night's lodging – most of the inhabitants were too old or too ill to work. The intention of Parliament that all paupers should be incarcerated was never carried out, since in 1880 twice as much was spent on 'out' relief in the county as on the unions.

The County Council became responsible for workhouses in 1930, but National Insurance, pensions, outdoor relief and coming of the Welfare State changed their functions, and they were turned into hostels, hospitals, old people's homes, private houses or were demolished.

Schools

The foundation of the earliest schools in Hertfordshire is not recorded In 1569 a free grammar school for 120 pupils was 'erected' by the corporation of St Albans in the Lady Chapel of the Abbey Church, but we know there was a flourishing school there 450 years earlier. One of the masters printed some of the earliest books in England, including the famous *Boke of Saint Albans*. At Stevenage a school is mentioned in 1312, and in 1558, the Reverend Thomas Alleyn left property to pay a teacher and to make statutes for its governance, and for prayers for himself as founder. All pupils had to converse in Latin, and were forbidden 'swareing or unhonest games or evill company of men or women or wenches'.

At Berkhamsted the school was founded by a 'brotherhood' of citizens about 1523, at the instigation of Dr Incent, former Dean of St Paul's. Barnet Grammar School followed in 1573 at the request of Robert, Earl of Leicester, and in 1579 the will of Margaret Dane to the Ironmongers Company of London included five pounds per year towards a school at Bishop's Stortford or to the poor. The Richard Platt school at Aldenham was endowed in 1595, and there were schools at Ware and Wareside in the early seventeenth century. Richard Hale founded the school at Hertford in 1616, and schools at Buntingford, Hitchin and Stanstead Abbots came into existence before 1650.

The best-known public school in Hertfordshire is Haileybury which was established by the East India Company for youths appointed to their service at Hertford Castle in 1804. The school moved to its impressive new premises near Little Amwell in 1806.

During the period 1698-1800 nineteen charity schools for elementary education were started along with numerous private schools – but many were 'dame schools' run by semi-illiterates to keep themselves out of the workhouse or plaiting schools, which were really sordid workshops. For the children of the labouring poor, Sunday schools began in 1785 and National Society schools in 1815 (by 1840 there were fifty). Many landowners built or contributed to elementary schools and in 1860 the county had one scholar to every 9.2 persons – above the national average. For the most part the interests of agriculture took precedence over education.

In 1872, only 78 of the 175 parishes provided enough school places under the Education Act but in 1877, 136 out of 147 School Board districts had sufficient suitable schools, though nine-tenths were provided by the voluntary sector. The voluntary system ended in 1902 when it had two-and-a-half times as many pupils as the board schools. In modern times, especially post-war, Hertfordshire has been held as an example to other authorities.

Nineteenth Century

Civil unrest and crime due mainly to low wages and near famine at the beginning of the nineteenth century prompted Parliament to consider taking law-enforcement out of the hands of the overworked parish constables, who, as the descendants of the early English tithingmen were elected, often unwillingly, to be responsible for not only law enforcement, but also the poor, weights and measures, conscription, statute fairs, licensing, punishments, repair of roads and bridges, collecting fines and taxes, and a host of other duties.

'Residents' Associations' of wealthy proprietors began to offer rewards for convictions, and in 1813 a constable was being maintained by private subscription at Barnet. The Watching and Lighting Act of 1833 permitted large towns to create their own forces, and in 1837 Hertford and St Albans constabularies were founded.

In 1836 a Royal Commission had reported: 'The depredations in some rural districts . . . threaten cultivation. It is not uncommon practice to lay open sheep folds and turn flocks loose at night . . . scarcely a week passed without sheep, pigs, poultry, corn or straw being stolen, generally with impunity.'

The Police Act of 1839 allowed the Justices to form a subcommittee to investigate the need for a county force. It found that seven parishes had no constable, and many others were inefficient. Amwell reported 'none but old Dogberries' and Watford 'the usual leet old women'.

There was opposition: the police would not be answerable to an elected body; the rural ratepayers would subsidise the towns. The Rector of Shenley said that police 'would be a ready instrument of tyranny and espionage' that would destroy 'what little simplicity is left to the rustics'! The County force was set up in 1841; St Albans Borough remained independent until 1947.

The Reform Bill of 1832 gave the county three seats in Parliament, and left the Boroughs with two each. A Parliamentary Commission in 1852 found that in St Albans election expenses since the Reform Act had been £37,000 – upwards of £24,600 having been spent on bribery, more than £3,000 per election, or £6 per vote cast! The town was disenfranchised by Act of Parliament.

There were frequent outbreaks of cholera, and public health became a concern. In 1848 Hitchin set up only the second Board of Health in England. That year 850 cases of typhus were reported with 162 deaths. There were only fifty-nine W.C.'s in the town, which had about 7,000 inhabitants.

Agriculture was improved by further enclosure. The Hertfordshire General Enclosure Act was passed in 1845 and another Act subsidised the laying of field drains. Chemical fertilisers came into use; John Bennet Lawes inherited the family estate at Rothamsted, near Harpenden, where he experimented on plant chemistry, and patented 'superphosphate'. From the income of this the world-famous Rothamsted Experimental Station was established.

Roads continued to improve in the nineteenth century. James MacAdam was surveyor to many turnpike trusts, and his father John Loudon was Surveyor General. He lived at Hoddesdon. In 1817 Telford was appointed to improve the Holyhead Road. It followed Watling street north of St Albans, but involved rerouting through the town, and south of Barnet. Telford produced a similar scheme for the Great North Road but there was much opposition to it from villages which it would have bypassed. The bill, drafted in 1829, never passed into law. Events overtook it in the shape of Stephenson's 'Rocket', which won the Rainhill Trials in that year at 30 mph. The Railway age had begun.

The first railway through the county, the London and Birmingham, followed the same route as the Grand Junction Canal, because it had the same destination, and

This dedication appeared on a map of Hertfordshire by John Warburton, an infamous Somerset herald, antiquarian and entrepreneur. Between 1716 and 1725 Warburton published maps of five counties with Middlesex, Essex and Hertfordshire on one sheet. These were based on new and original surveys making Warburton's contribution an important influence in county mapping. The Hertfordshire map, as shown here, was published individually in 1749 and was used as the basis for most maps of the county for the next forty years. (By courtesy of the British Library)

The Grove, a tunnel over a mile long was dug, and a 40 foot embankment created south of it. This tunnel cost ten lives. The Tring cutting involved forty-three accidents requiring hospital treatment, six of them fatal. The line reached Tring in October 1837, and Birmingham in 1838.

The second main line followed the other navigable water, up the Lea valley. The North-Eastern Railway was intended to go to Yarmouth via Cambridge, but lack of funds and opposition by landowners shortened it. It reached Broxbourne in 1840, Bishop's Stortford in 1842 and Hertford in 1843.

The Great North Road had been produced by cobbling together existing minor roads at the end of the seventeenth century. It was not a logical, planned route, but it had been responsible for the growth of towns through the centre of the county. The Great Northern Railway engineers, wishing to create a parallel route to York, faced a daunting task of construction made even more difficult by opposition

required a low gradient. To satisfy this, a cutting 2¼ miles long and 57 feet deep was made at Tring, very like the one for the nearby canal.

Railways, unlike canals, could not be looked upon as landscape improvements, and, to avoid Cassiobury and

from landowners. Prevented from taking a route along the Mimram valley, they took a line between the country seats at Lockleys and Tewin Water. Here Brassey and Cubitt built a viaduct 1560 feet long and 100 feet high which is the major industrial monument in the county. The line was opened to Peterborough in 1850.

The Midland Railway was originally a provincial system which shared lines with the London and Birmingham Railway in order to provide services to the capital. In 1853 a better offer was made by the Great Northern, allowing use of their track from Hitchin, which became a major junction when the connection from Wigston through Bedfordshire was completed in 1857. The GNR, however, always gave priority to their own trains, and charged the Midland £60,000 a year. After the Silver Jubilee exhibition, when many Midland specials were delayed, the Midland Railway planned the route via St Albans to St Pancras, which was opened in 1868.

Many branch lines were constructed at the whim of landowners and speculators. Several were planned and authorised but never built, and some were drawn in anticipation by cartographers who were caught out by rapid changes of landscape. The pattern of the main lines was similar to that of the roads: radial from London. If you were prepared to change trains several times (or, like Lord Salisbury of Hatfield, had your own train and lots of money and influence), there were some cross-country routes, but it was usually easier to go into London and come back out. At the beginning of this century committee meetings of the County Council were held, for convenience, in London!

A cross-country railway was planned from Dunstable and Luton to Hertford. The Great Northern Railway would not allow it to cross its main line, however, and a double junction was therefore made south of Digswell Viaduct. Called, for no good reason, Welwyn Junction (it lay just south of the parish of Digswell, in the parish of Hatfield), it marked the site where Welwyn Garden City was to be created sixty years later, and was probably responsible for the name, but not the location, of the new town.

The railway changed the character of the county to an enormous degree. It did more to destroy 'what simplicity remained to the rustics' than any police force. It made it possible to send fresh produce to the London Market from almost anywhere in the county. It brought the ideas and products of industrial revolution – for instance coal replaced wood in fireplaces. It enabled people to make journeys hitherto unimaginable because they had been unable to afford either the time or the money. Above all, it made it possible to commute from the country to the city daily.

Droving ceased and cattle markets were held instead. The Rev. J Clutterbuck, a curate at Watford, wrote in the *Journal of the Royal Agricultural Society* in 1864:

'The modern practice of sales of fat stock by auction at such towns as Hitchin, Hertford, Bishop's Stortford and Watford has assumed large and increased proportions. (At Hitchin) sales, held occasionally in 1852 took place in 1853 three times a month, and, ultimately, in 1853 every week.'

Perishable goods could be transported over great distances; milk churns and hampers of watercress were everyday sights on railway stations all over the county, and market gardening, already established, became a major industry. By the end of the century the Lea valley contained one-quarter of the acreage of glasshouses in the country, producing cucumbers, grapes, flowers, foliage plants and tomatoes.

The centres of gravity of settlements often shifted closer to the stations, as at Knebworth, Hitchin and Hemel Hempstead. Towns close to the metropolis, where workers could commute, grew mainly by addition of houses and those further out by the development of light, usually agriculturally based, industries and the homes of the workers employed by them.

Watford was changed to an astonishing degree. To Daniel Defoe, in 1724, the town, which had been created as a market in the late twelfth century, was still 'a genteel market town . . . having but one street' and it was described in similar terms for another hundred years. The canal reached the town in 1801, and the railway in 1837. Its population grew at seven times the rate of the rest of the county during the second half of the century. In 1801 the population of Watford was 3,530 and in 1901, 32,559. Today it is over 80,000.

Before 1845 Hertfordshire was divided between two dioceses: London and Lincoln – and split between scattered archdeaconries. In 1845 there was a rationalisation and Hertfordshire was put into the diocese of Rochester, of all places! In 1875 a new diocese was created, and the Abbey, which had been a parish church, became a cathedral (al-though the enthronement was not until 1877). The great building is, correctly, the Cathedral and Abbey Church of St Alban. In the same year the borough was granted a royal charter which, by a slip of grammar, makes it not St Alban's City, but the City of St Albans.

County Industry

The *Victoria County History* at the beginning of the twentieth century said of Watford: 'The comparative cheapness of land and the good railway facilities have resulted in the erection of a number of factories and works.' Its comments on homes reveal a nice social distinction:

> 'Houses of smaller description . . . have attracted a large number of workers engaged in London. . . . The residential portion . . . lies to the north of the town. It is well timbered and contains many pleasant residences with large gardens, mostly occupied by gentlemen engaged in business in London.'

When the 'workers' left their 'houses of smaller description' very early in the morning they used cheap workmen's tickets. The 'gentlemen' left later, using first-class passes which were included with the purchase of their 'pleasant residences' and were valid for twenty-one years.

Without metal ores or fossil fuels, the county had to wait for bulk transport by the canal and the railways before it had its industrial revolution. Malting, brewing and milling were its main industries, along with 'forest industries' producing wooden tools, treen, hurdles and baskets.

In malting, barley is soaked and then allowed to germinate, turning starch into malt, a mixture of sugars which can be fermented into alcohol. The process, simple in principle, was skilled in practice, and from early times was carried out in maltings, where the grain could be spread out to an optimum thickness and turned by hand. As soon as the germination had reached exactly the right stage, the grain was roasted in kilns. Many towns had maltings for local use and

The viaduct at Digswell near Welwyn was an amazing feat of engineering. It consists of forty arches and was built in 1848-50 to carry the Great Northern Railway across the valley of the river Mimram. It is about 1560 feet (475 metres) long and about 98 feet (30 metres) high. (Photo by Tony Rook)

in the north-east of the county there were large numbers. Easily recognisable by their size and oast-like kilns, they are now threatened industrial monuments, since a deep fluidised-bed process is now used by brewers. Brewing, once a home industry (there were seventy-nine in St Albans in 1355!) also became centralised. In the eighteenth century there were fifty local breweries in Hertfordshire, in addition to thousands of houses with licenses to brew. Today McMullen's of Hertford is the sole survivor.

During the nineteenth century, largely because of the revolution in and war with France, straw plaiting became a major cottage industry here, the plaits being sewn together to form hats at Luton. The trade had a great social impact. Most of the plaiters were female, and could earn more than an agricultural labourer. The work could also be done in spare time in addition to other employment in the fields. A poor crop of wheat meant a good crop of straw and plaiting made the people more independent and helped, to some degree, to even out the effects of fluctuations in corn prices.

Water mills were not only used for flour; other materials could be ground and water power could be used for other industries, especially sawing wood. 'Stocking' mills were used for fulling cloth, a process by which wet woollen material was 'trodden' by mechanical feet or stocks to bulk or 'full' it. The stocks could be adapted for making paper pulp

from rags. Many mills changed use several times. In the eighteenth century paper-making was well established in the west of the county. In 1804 the troubles in France which had added to the success of the straw hat makers, also brought the Fourdriniers with their continuous papermaking process to the county, at Frogmore. The process was improved by a stationer, John Dickinson. He had six paper mills in the county the largest covering thirty acres. His daughter married John Evans, best known for archaeological research in Britain, and their son, Arthur who discovered the Minoan civilisation, and used his fortune to restore Knossos.

The only extractive industries in the county until this century were of chalk to spread on the fields and to make lime; the flint from the chalk for building and glassmaking; Totterwhoe Stone, a hard chalk rock once used in buildings, which was actually mined near Ashwell and Dunstable; clay for brick and tilemaking as well as pottery, mainly in the Roman and medieval periods, and 'coprolites' (phosphatic nodules from the gault clay) which were used to make superphosphate at Ashwell until this century.

The extensive use of concrete more recently has led to massive extraction of gravel. The pits are later exploited either as amenities for fishing, water sports or reserves, or, more profitably, as holes into which waste can be dumped.

During the nineteenth century an experiment was tried in 'new town' development that is all but forgotten today, although remnants of it can still be seen. In May 1846, Feargus O'Connor, founder of the National Charter Association, bought 103 acres of agricultural land at Heronsgate near Chorleywood for £2,344. Foremost in opposing violence as a way of getting political reform, he sought another solution, that of enfranchising many people by replacing few great landowners with many small ones.

The land was divided into small plots, with cottages and

outbuildings for livestock. There was a school but no church or public house. Tenants of O'Connorsville were to be given freehold by lot from 70,000 subscribers, and money for seed and stock. Each would also receive the vote. Like privatisation today, it was an attempt to make people change sides in a political struggle. O'Connor's opponents in Parliament soon had the lottery declared illegal. They pointed out that proper accounts were not kept, although they admitted that O'Connor had been subsidising the scheme from his own pocket. In any case, the scheme was not financially viable and the company was bankrupt and closed by Act of Parliament in 1851. After a scene in the House of Commons, O'Connor was kept in an asylum until his death in 1854. The houses he built are now much sought-after in a rural area of Metroland and close to the M25.

The first real new town after the creation of the medieval markets was Letchworth Garden City. Ebenezer Howard, whose brainchild it was, was neither sociologist nor architect; but a self-taught stenographer and the son of a baker and confectioner in the East End.

Sydney Low had written, in *Contemporary Review* in 1891:

'The centre of population is shifting from the heart to the limbs. The life blood is pouring into the long arms of brick and mortar and cheap stucco that are feeling their way out into . . . the Hertfordshire copses . . . The people of London will dwell in urban sanitary districts straggling far down into the Home Counties.'

Howard saw a solution to the problems caused by the continuous growth of the metropolis that had been made possible by improved transport, trams and trains.

In 1898 he published a small book: *Tomorrow – A Peaceful Path to Real Reform*. In it he wrote:

'There are in reality not only, as is so constantly assumed, two alternatives – town life and country life – but a third alternative, in which all the advantages of the most energetic and active town life, with all the beauty and delight of the country, may be secured in perfect combination.'

Of course, by this time the right to vote was not at issue (for men, that is). Howard did not have the ideal of artisans becoming smallholders either; he intended that industry and housing should grow together. His idea had something in common with O'Connor's: the common good which was to be served.

'All ground rents, which are to be based on the annual value of the land, shall be paid to the Trustees, who, after providing for interest and the sinking fund, will hand the balance to the Central Council of the new municipality, to be employed . . . in the maintenance of all necessary public works – roads, schools, parks etc.'

The amazing thing was the speed and enthusiasm with which the scheme was taken up. In 1899, Howard addressed a meeting of fewer than twenty people, which formed a Garden City Association. In 1902 the Pioneer Company was founded, and work began on Letchworth Garden City. Eighteen years later Welwyn Garden City was begun.

The Garden Cities provided the pattern which today seems so commonplace: a townscape with wide grass verges lined with trees, cottage-style dwellings, adequate gardens – the inspiration for between-the-wars suburbia.

Howard's book contained a diagram of the central city surrounded by a ring of garden cities, linked by radial and peripheral roads and railways. G.R. Taylor coined the expression 'satellite towns'. The example, surprisingly, was not taken up by government. Housing was left to private developers and district councils, although the London County Council obtained Green Belt legislation in 1938. A Royal Commission set up to study the problem did not report until after the beginning of the war, and the Greater London Plan was published in 1944. It suggested ten sites for satellite towns, and in 1946 the New town Act was passed. Stevenage was designated in October and Hemel Hempstead in February of the next year. Hatfield with Welwyn Garden City followed in 1948.

In the 1920's an advertisement for Welwyn Garden City read:

'It is not good to waste two hours daily in trains, buses and trams to and from the workshop, leaving no time for leisure and recreation. At Welwyn Garden City a man's house will be near his work in a pure and healthy atmosphere. He will have time and energy after his work for leisure and recreation.'

The creation of industry and housing in the town was never in step, however, and it was a dormitory for London commuters from the start.

The ideals of Garden Cities and New Towns were overtaken by the motor car. When they began nobody could foresee how easy it would become for workers to travel. Today Hertfordshire, with its pleasant towns, villages and hamlets, each surrounded by its green belt of readily accessible countryside is all Garden City – the Garden City of England *for delight!*

Famous Names in Herts

A large number of outstanding people have been associated with the county. Sir Henry Chauncy, the historian, distinguished 'the most worthy Knights and Esquires' from 'People whereof the greatest part were Men of small Value and no Substance'. Such matters were easier in his day, perhaps, but even he lists some eighty names of the former at the time of Henry VI, as well as about five hundred sheriffs. As observed in the text, lesser gentlemen came and went here as nowhere else, throughout history. This is intended as a short list of men of note for their achievements rather than their substance. Many people have no doubt been forgotten, and at least seventy-two poets have been omitted from the list for reasons of space.

As there were two royal castles and many royal estates in Hertfordshire, so many monarchs have been born, imprisoned and made welcome at residences in the county, that kings and queens, English and foreign, have not been included. However, many people will know that Elizabeth Bowes-Lyon, the Queen Mother, was brought up at St Paul's Walden.

ALBAN. Died 293 A.D.	Protomatyr	St Albans
ANSON, Lord George 1697-1762	Navigator	Moor Park
ASHMOLE, Elias 1617-92	Antiquary	E. Barnet
BACON, Sir Nicholas 1509-1579	Keeper of Great Seal, Statesman	St Albans
BACON, Sir Francis 1561-1626, Baron Verulam, Viscount	Philosopher, Essayist, Chancellor	St Albans
BALIOL, John De. Died 1269	Founded Oxford College	Hitchin
BECKETT, Thomas 1117-70	Archbishop of Canterbury Martyr	Bramfield
BENSTEDE, Sir John de. Died 1323?	Chancellor 1306-7	Benington
BERNERS, Dame f 1486	Wrote *Boke of St Albans*	St Albans
BESSEMER Sir Henry 1813-98	Inventor	Hitchin
BREAKSPEAR, Nicholas. Died 1159	Pope Adrian IV	Abbots Langley
BRIDGEWATER Duke Francis 1736-1803	Canal Builder	Ashridge
CECIL William 1520-98 Lord Burghley	Chief Minister	Hatfield
CECIL Robert 1563-1612 Earl of Salisbury	Chief Minister	Theobalds
CECIL Robert 1830-1903 Marquess of Salisbury	Prime Minister	Hatfield
CHAPMAN, George 1559-1627	Translated Homer, Poet	Hitchin
CHAUNCY, Charles 1592-1627	President of Harvard	Ardley & Ware
CHAUNCY, Sir Henry 1632-1719	County Historian	Ardley
CHAUCER, Geoffrey 1343?-1400	Poet	Berkhampstead
CHERRY-GARRARD, Apsley	Antarctic Explorer	Wheathampstead
CLIVE, Lord Robert 1725-74	Clive of India	Hemel Hempstead
CLUTTERBUCK, Robert 1772-1831	Historian	Watford
COWPER, Earl William 1664-1723	Lord Chancellor	Panshanger
COWPER, William 1731-1800	Poet	Berkhamsted
CRUDEN, Alexander 1701-70	Wrote Concordance	Ware
CUMMINGS, Sir Alexander. Died 1775	Indian Chief	Barnet
DIMSDALE Thomas 1712-1800	Innoculator	Hertford
EDGEWORTH, Maria 1767-1849	Novelist	Northchurch
ELIOT, John 1604-90	Apostle to Indians	Widford
EVANS, Sir John 1823-1908	Antiquary	Berkhamsted
EVANS, Sir Arthur 1851-1941	Archaeologist	Berkhamsted
FANSHAWE, Sir Robert, 1608-66	Diplomat & Poet	Ware
FRANCLIN, Thomas 1701-70	Translater	Ware, Thundridge
GADDESDEN, John of. Died c. 1350	Court Physician	Ltl Gaddesden
GAVESTON, Piers. Died 1312	Royal Favourite	Berkhamsted
GODWIN, William 1756-86	Novelist, Historian	Ware
GORDON, William 1728-1807	Historian of USA	Hitchin
GREENE, Grahame 1904-	Novelist	Berkhamsted
GRESLEY, Sir Nigel 1876-1941	Locomotive Designer	Salisbury Hall
GUNTER, Edmund 1581-1626	Surveyor, Navigator	Hertford
GWYNNE, Nell 1650-91	Royal Mistress	Tring & Salisbury Hall
HADLEY, John. Died 1744	Invented the Sextant	E. Barnet
HERRING, Thomas 1693-1757	Archbishop of York & Canterbury	Barley
HOWARD, Ebenezer 1850-1928	Town Planner	Letchworth, WGC
HOWE, Richard 1725-99	Lord of Admiralty	Shenley
KEN, Thomas 1634-1711	Bishop of Bath & Wells	Ltl Berkhampstead
LAMB, Charles 1775-1834	Poet and Essayist	Several Places
LAWES, John 1839-81	Agricultural Scientist	Rothamsted
LYTTON, Edward Bulwer 1803-73	Dilettante, Author	Knebworth
LYTTON, Edward Robert 1831-91	Politician, Author	Knebworth
MACADAM, John, 1756-1836	Road Maker	Hoddesdon
MACAULEY, Baron Thomas 1800-1859	Historian	Aspenden
MASKELYNE, Viscount Nevil 1732-1811	Astronomer Royal	Barnet
MALTHUS, Rev Thomas 1766-1834	Economist	Haileybury
MELBOURNE, Viscount William (Lamb) 1779-1848	Statesman	Brocket Hall

MONTFORT, Simon de. c. 1200-65	Statesman, soldier	Ware
MOORE, Henry 1898-1986	Sculptor	Much Hadham
MORE, Sir Thomas 1480-34	Chancellor, author	North Mimms
MORECAMBE, Eric 1926-1982	Comedian	Harpenden
MORELL, Thomas 1703-84	Librettist for Handel	Buckland
NEVILLE, George. c. 1433-1476	Lord Chancellor and Archibishop of Exeter, York	Moor Park
NOWELL, Alexander 1507-1602	Author of the Catechism	Much Hadham
ORWELL, George (Eric Blair) 1903-1950	Author	Wallington
PALMERSTON, Viscount Henry1784-1865	Statesman	Brocket Hall
PARIS, Matthew. Died 1259	Historian	St Albans
PENN, William 1644-1718	Founded Pennsylvania	Chorleywood
PRYOR, Alfred 1839-81	County Botanist	Hatfield, Baldock
RHODES, Cecil 1853-1902	Founded Rhodesia	Bishop's Stortford
ROTHSCHILD, Baron Lionel 1868-1937	Naturalist	Tring
SADLIER, Sir Ralph 1507-87	Counsellor to Eliz I	Standon
SALMON, Nathaniel 1675-1742	County Historian	Westmill, Stotford
SHAW, George Bernard 1856-1950	Playwright	Ayot St Lawrence
SOMERS, Baron John c. 1650-1716	Lawyer, Statesman	Brookmans Park
TEMPLE, Sir William 1628-99	Statesman, Diplomat	Bishop's Stortford
TERRY, Dame Ellen 1847-1928	Actress	Harpenden
TRADESCANT, John. Died? 1637	Gardener	Hatfield
TROLLOPE, Anthony 1815-82	Novellist	Waltham Cross
VILLIERS, George 1800-70 (Earl Clarendon)	Envoy to Madrid Lord Lieutenant Ireland	The Grove, Watford
WALTON, Izaac 1593-1683	Wrote Compleat Angler	Lea Valley
WARD, Seth 1618-89	Prof. of Astronomy Bishop of Exeter, Salisbury	Buntingford
WARD, Mrs Humphrey 1851-1920	1st Woman Magistrate, Novelist	Aldbury
WAREHAM, William. Died 1532	Archbishop of Canterbury	Barley
WATTS, Isaac 1674-1748	Hymn writer	Theobalds
WESTALL, Richard 1765-1836	RA, taught Queen Victoria to paint	Hertford
WOLSEY, Thomas 1471-1530	Cardinal, Statesman	Gt Wymondley, Moor Pk
WOOD, Sir Henry 1869-1944	Conductor	Chorleywood, Stevenage
YOUNG, Edward 1684-1765	Poet	Welwyn

Bibliography

*Books with extensive bibliographies

Addison, Sir William. *The Old Roads of England* (Batsford) 1980

Bailey, Brian J. *Portrait of Hertfordshire* (Robert Hale) 1978

Barton, P. *The Peasants' Revolt in Hertfordshire* (Hertfordshire Publications) 1981

Bowden, R.A. *Genealogical Sources* (County Record Office) 1972

Branigan, K. *Town and Country* (Spurbooks) 1973

Chauncy, Sir Henry. *Historical Antiquities of Hertfordshire* 1700 (Reprinted Kohler & Coombes) 1975

Davis, K. Rutherford. *Britons and Saxons* (Phillimore) 1982

Davis, K. Rutherford. *Deserted Medieval Villages* (Phillimore) 1973

Defoe, D. *Tour Through the Whole Island of Great Britain* (two-vols Cass 1927, Ed. Rogers, Penguin) 1724

Dony, J.G. *A History of the Straw Hat Industry* (Gibb Banforth) 1942

Ellis, W. *Practical Farming . . .* 1732

Evans, H. *The New Towns . . .* (TCPA) 1972

Evans, Ifor and Lawrence, Heather. *Christopher Saxton, Elizabethan Mapmaker* (Wakefield Historical Publications) 1979

Faulkner, A.H. *The Grand Union Canal in Hertfordshire* (Hertfordshire Publications) 1988

Gough, J.W. *Sir Hugh Middleton* (Clarendon) 1964

Hertfordshire Archaeology

Hertfordshire Countryside

Hertfordshire Past and Present

Hertfordshire's Past

Hodson, Donald. *Four County Maps of Hertfordshire . . . with Introductions* (Hertfordshire Publications) 1985

Hodson, Donald. *Printed Maps of Hertfordshire 1577-1900* (Dawsons of Pall Mall) 1974

Johnson, W. Branch. *The Industrial Archaeology of Hertfordshire* (David and Charles) 1970

Johnson, W. Branch. *Hertfordshire* (Batsford) 1970

Johnson, W. Branch. *Local History in Hertfordshire* (Hertfordshire Local History Council) 1964*

Jones, Arthur. *Hertfordshire Shire County Guide 18* (Shire Publications) 1988

Kingstone, A. *Hertfordshire During the Great Civil War* (Stephen Austin) 1894

Le Hardy, W. *Guide to the Hertfordshire Record Office* (CRO) 1961

Moreland, Carl and Bonnister, D. *Antique Maps* (Longman) 1983

Morris, J. (ed) *Domesday Book, Hertfordshire* (Phillimore) 1976

Moss-Eccardt, J. *Ebenezer Howard* (Shire) 1974

Page, W. (ed) *The Victoria County History, Hertfordshire* 1906-1914* (reprinted London University) 1975

Pahl, R.E. *Urbs in Rure* (LSE) 1965

Pevsner, N. *The Buildings of England: Hertfordshire* (Penquin) 1977

Renn, D. *Medieval Castles in Hertfordshire* (Phillimore) 1971
Robert, R. *Historic Hertfordshire* (Hertfordshire Countryside) 1968
Robert, R. *Famous Authors in Hertfordshire* (Hertfordshire Countryside) 1970
Robinson. *Guide to County History III – Hertfordshire* (Barracuda) 1978*
Rook, Tony. *Welwyn Beginning* (Author) 1968
Rook, Tony. *A History of Hertfordshire* (Phillimore) 1984*
Rook, Tony. *A History of Hertfordshire's Roads* (Author) 1989
Shirley, D. (ed) *Hertfordshire: A Guide to the Countryside* (Egon) 1978
Swinson, A. *The Quest for Alban* (Friends of St Albans Abbey) 1971
Thwaite, M.F. *Periodicals and Transactions relating to Hertfordshire* (Hertfordshire Local History Council) 1959*
Toms, E. *The Story of St Albans* (White Crescent) 1975
Transactions of The East Hertfordshire Archaeological Society
Transactions of The St Albans Architectural and Archaeological Society
Walker, D. *A General View of the Agriculture of Hertfordshire* 1785
Young, A. *A General View of the Agriculture of Hertfordshire* 1804 (reprinted David and Charles) 1971

Acknowledgements

Our grateful thanks are due to Simon Pointer of Map House for the loan of maps; Donald Hodson for his advice, Tessa Campbell for helping with picture research, and the staff of the County Record Office and County Library for their friendly and patient help throughout.

Information about the authors

Valerie Scott is editor of a quarterly journal called *The Map Collector*, which is read by early map enthusiasts all over the world. She also runs a company called Map Collector Publications Ltd. which publishes books on the history of maps and mapping, and is editor of an in-flight magazine *Air 2000*. Her previous books in this county history series are *Buckinghamshire*, *Berkshire* and *Sussex*. She is a Fellow of the Royal Geographical Society and holds the International Map Collectors' Society award for her work in the history of cartography. Her home is at Tring in Hertfordshire.

Tony Rook also lives in Hertfordshire at Welwyn. While a schoolboy at The Judd, Tonbridge, he became an experienced archaeological excavator. After regular service in the RAF as a radar specialist he read science at Leicester where he was Convenor of Debates, editor of *Lucifer*, met his wife, Merle, and received his bachelor's degree. After six years as a research scientist he was for ten years Head of Science at Sherrardswood School where he directed the excavation of a Roman villa and the preservation of its baths under the motorway. He was awarded the degree of Master of Philosophy for his research in archaeology. He is a member of the Institute of Field Archaeology and a Fellow of the Society of Antiquaries of London, and an extramural tutor in archaeology for London and Cambridge universities. His published works include two novels, the 'Rookbook' educational models, and a *History of Hertfordshire* which he wrote and illustrated.

The first balloon flight in England, which started at Finsbury, ended at Standon Green End in the county. A large sandstone boulder marks the spot today and bears the legend telling the story for 'posterity'. The balloonist was Vincent Lunardi, Secretary to the Neapolitan Ambassador in London, and the flight took place on September 15, 1784 and lasted two hours. It is interesting to speculate on the amazement of the local populace when this apparition appeared in the sky! This drawing is in the Oldfield Collection (p.95 Vol 6). (By courtesy of Herts County Record Office)